GW00480786

WRITE

—— LIKE A ——

THOUGHT
LEADER

How to find a constant stream of story ideas
to position yourself as the go-to expert
in your niche

RHEA WESSEL

Writer and Founder, The Institute for Thought Leadership

whose work has appeared in

The New York Times, The Wall Street Journal and the BBC

ISBN: 978-0-9970625-2-6 (softcover)
ISBN: 978-0-9970625-5-7 (hardcover)
ISBN: 978-0-9970625-3-3 (ebook)
ISBN: 978-0-9970625-6-4 (audiobook)

Published by The Idea Producers
Rhea Wessel
Schreyerstr. 57
61476 Kronberg im Taunus, Germany
www.theideaproducers.com
www.instituteforthoughtleadership.com
www.rheawessel.com

Cover design by Mexelina™
Interior design and ebook by Jill Ronsley

*To all the experts out there
who have great ideas the world needs to hear ...
And the one who is closest to my heart*

Contents

PART 1
Find Your Thought-Leadership Niche

PART 2
Find Your Thought-Leadership Stories

PART 3
Flesh It Out: Expand on Your Ideas in Writing

List of Figures

My Journey With This Book

I wrote this book because I love ideas, and I love to help people make their ideas sing.

For as long as I can remember, I have been fascinated by good ideas—the kind that give me a zing when they come into focus, and the ones that open new possibilities for the future.

"Write Like a Thought Leader" is not only about writing, ideation and story-finding, it's also about my personal journey of creating this book and getting to the point where I am in my life and work.

Until recently, I didn't perceive myself as someone who might have something authoritative to say. I had chosen to work as a reporter and writer, sharing about other people's ideas, not my own.

I had found a safe place as the one who asked the questions, not the one who answered them.

Then, as I brainstormed for this book, I realized I could fill the shoes of the expert instead of just the reporter.

There's more to that story, though.

When I was growing up in the 1970s in Texas, using the wrong words or the wrong tone brought draconian penalties and harsh punishment. Looking back at this now, I realize those punishments left lifelong scars.

Since I began to associate slips of the tongue with punishment, I didn't fully express myself as a young adult and later as an employee or a romantic partner. I felt trapped inside myself, unable to articulate verbally what I wanted to say, and afraid of the consequences if I did.

As a journalist, the tables occasionally got turned on me, and it was terrifying. As a young reporter for Dow Jones, I had to appear on CNBC and answer the anchor's questions about the markets. I was way out of my comfort zone.

For a good 25 years, I did little or no public speaking and found it very difficult to begin with even small things like making my first YouTube videos or giving a presentation at a conference. I was much more comfortable having a conversation with a blank piece of paper.

When I began this project to write a book about thought leadership, I didn't expect it to transform me as a person or to transform my business the way it has. I was going at it as a reporter. I had planned to report on, synthesize, and present the ideas of others.

Yet, this book has turned out to be deeply personal, and the writing of it launched me on my mission to help the experts of this world find and frame their best ideas to solve some of Earth's biggest problems. My personal story helps me understand how I landed with this goal.

In a certain sense, after my childhood experiences, I have come full circle by helping others fully express themselves and be heard. This book and my work is an expression of my personal story of transformation.

With that in mind, here's a bit of a warning: This isn't your standard writing book.

It is a writing book that is the result of years of self-discovery work done simultaneously with efforts to master my craft writing for top global publications, including the BBC, The Wall Street Journal and The New York Times.

It's a work in progress that, like any good story, may have many updates and editions to come. In 2019, as I launched on the writing phase, I was only partly aware of what would turn up on the following pages. As a journalist, I knew I must follow the story wherever it takes me. And that's what I did here—even though it's my own story, in part.

This book is for subject-matter experts who want to have a bigger impact with their ideas and their work. They are driven by purpose and passion and seek a greater good.

Therefore, I'd like to begin by saying this: As an expert in your niche, we need you to be speaking out and contributing to the conversation and the solutions. This world has big problems, but we already have many of the solutions we need to solve them.

It is our own responsibility to get our ideas into the world, and I hope this book helps you do just that in a bigger, better and more sophisticated way.

As you do, you will serve your audience and all who come after you.

And, in the process, you'll begin to reach your higher potential.

That is your main reward.

Introduction

With all the hype around content and "content marketing," companies and individuals know they need to produce written materials that are of high value and interest to their readers.

They want to present themselves as experts in a specific niche—as thought leaders—but they are unsure how to do it. In my experience as a journalist and now as a writer for companies, I know that even the best and brightest struggle to tell a story from a fresh angle. Instead, they write articles that are salesy, dry, or read like a study.

Other frequent problems in writing that is meant to be in the thought-leadership style include:

- being afraid to give away your knowledge and therefore saying little or nothing of value in an article
- trying to appeal to high-level readers but talking down to them instead
- missing the chance to tell a bigger story
- choosing poor story angles and thereby losing the chance to tell the story at all

Because of poor writing and an uninteresting story angle—the most frequent problem—companies and individuals squander the chance to be seen as thought leaders.

In some cases, the writing is so uninspiring, or the story says something that is so obvious and well known, that the writer or the company publishing the story actually does the opposite of what is intended: Instead of gaining the reader's trust, they begin to lose it.

You may have picked up this book because you or the people in your company who are writing struggle with some of the points I mentioned. Or perhaps you bought it because you're just not so sure what to write about.

Nursing your ideas

Maybe you're sitting on a good idea like a hen on her nest. You are brooding over your idea, but you're scared to let it take flight. Indeed, this is the writer's curse: Once words are down on paper, you lose a certain amount of control over them. And there's always an inherent fear of failure. That fear can be stifling and is partly what makes writing a risky enterprise.

Shortly before I went on my first writing retreat to create this book, I saw a film that was, in essence, based on a book I wrote.

My narrative nonfiction manuscript, about the life and death of Hatun Sürücü, a Kurdish-German woman murdered by her youngest brother in Berlin in 2005, still sits in my desk drawer. For many writers, having their manuscript turned into a film is the crowning achievement. But, alas, the film I saw wasn't based on my work. One reason is because I succumbed to self-doubt. I listened to the judge in my head who said I wasn't up to the mighty task of narrative nonfiction.

If you're a hen on your nest like I was, and you have ideas that need to be told, I hope this book can help you give those ideas wing. If you're working with sensitive material, I hope it helps you find the right way to frame the story so that it has your desired impact.

Five types of thought-leadership writing

There are five types of thought-leadership writing. In the short form, a body of work can add up to thought-leadership writing.

They are:

- **Short-form, first-person articles**
  - Such as LinkedIn articles (not posts), Medium articles or blogs
- **Magazine-length reported stories**
  - Feature-style reported articles based on research and multiple interviews. Includes quotes. May include data.
- **In-depth interviews**
  - Deep-dive interviews, presented in writing in Q&A format
- **Studies**
  - Studies on an industry, process, product or service. Based on proprietary data or unique viewpoint/synthesis. Studies can be thought-leadership writing on their own.
- **Books**
  - Books about a subject-matter that present it in a new and fresh way. Books can be thought-leadership writing on their own.

"Write Like a Thought Leader" specifically focuses on short-form articles, but the ideas can be applied to all lengths of writing.

Overview of book structure

Writing in the thought-leadership style comes down to how you tell the story.

That "how," in a broad sense, is the subject of this book.

In Part 1 (Chapters 1-5), we look at finding and articulating your own thought-leadership niche.

In Part 2 (Chapter 6), the focus is on finding the right angle for stories born out of your thought-leadership niche. Finding the right angle is a process I call story framing.

Part 3 (Chapters 7-8) is about the execution of well-framed stories in writing. It includes definitions of the types of thought-leadership stories, examples and my tips and tricks.

Most likely, you didn't pick up this book because you're working on book-length narrative nonfiction, like I did years ago.

Most likely, you're interested in sharing your ideas that relate to your business. Perhaps you intend to publish these ideas on your blog, or as articles for LinkedIn or Medium. Maybe you are a freelancer, a coach, a trainer, a small business owner, an asset manager, a scientist, or employed by a knowledge-based company, like a consultancy or a law or accounting firm.

In any of these cases, you may be worried about how your writing comes across to readers and whether it reflects the depth of your thought and the richness of your experience. You may have great ideas but struggle to get them heard within or outside the organization.

Instead of being the visible expert you could and should be, you're an invisible expert, or at least it feels that way sometimes.

Or, in the worst case, you may be concerned that your writing may be used against you in the court of public opinion.

When an individual has the courage to get out there and share their thinking about a matter that's important to them, that's to be congratulated. But unfortunately, sometimes it leads to being ridiculed, which makes one more reticent to even try.

What's in it for you?

As a journalist, I usually think in story. When I see a subject, meet a person, or hear an idea that intrigues me, I'm already thinking of the headline for my story. It is simply normal for me to see the landscape around me as fertile ground for finding stories. This is how most of the journalists I know think.

While viewing the world in story mode may not be natural to you, I'd like for you to start thinking like a journalist in your field or business, actively seeking out not just any old story but the right story to tell. I believe you will find so many stories waiting in the wings. They are stories that want to be found. Stories that want to be written.

I'm not promising to save you from all humiliation and criticism that some commentators may put you through, but what I can do is help you gain confidence with the following:

- You are writing material that you're best-suited to write.
  - Part 1 is about finding your thought-leadership niche.
- You are approaching the ideas with a fresh viewpoint and bringing the conversation forward, instead of allowing it to stagnate.
  - Part 2 of is about framing your story.

- And you are using tried-and-true journalistic techniques that result in writing that is conversational, lively and easy to read.
  - Part 3 is about fleshing out your story.

Introducing the three-step process to thought-leadership writing

Thought-leadership writing is a three-step process I have defined: Find It, Frame It, and Flesh It Out. (See Figure 1.) I will lead you through these three steps.

Three steps to thought-leadership writing

Figure 1—Three steps to thought-leadership writing

Since thought-leadership writing is a process, and most ideas in this book build upon others, I strongly recommend reading this work from top to bottom. If you try to skip through the chapters and look for what a marketing person might call "snackable" content, you may find some nuggets that whet your appetite. But the rest may seem out of context because you haven't gone on the journey with me from the beginning.

My goal

My goal with this process and this book is to inspire you to take your ideas out to the world. I want to equip all those who have ideas they're burning to express with the tools they need to craft a better story.

Specifically, I want to teach you the process of framing your ideas into stories that serve the needs of your readers.

It doesn't matter if your ideas are about optimizing the supply chain, factor investing, or tending beehives. The subject is nearly irrelevant. Making your ideas interesting and useful to your reader is about how you frame them.

How this book emerged

How did all this get its start?

When I began this writing journey, I had set out with the vague goal of writing something about thought leadership. It was a term gaining buzzword status, and I felt attracted.

I went out and bought every book online that had the words "thought leadership" in the title and got to reading. I was impressed, especially by the book by Matt Church and his co-authors Peter Cook and Scott Stein, called "The Thought Leaders Practice," and by that of Denise Brosseau, called "Ready to Be a Thought Leader? How to Increase your Influence, Impact and Success."

My goal with this process and this book is to inspire you to take your ideas out to the world. I want to equip all those who have ideas they're burning to express with the tools they need to craft a better story.

At first, I thought there wasn't much way to contribute to the conversation because the existing books had done such a good job with it. But then I realized that most books about thought leadership focus on how to find and articulate the area in which you want to be seen as an authority and how to codify your knowledge into nuggets of intellectual property.

Very few books discuss the framing and writing of thought-leadership materials.

If they do, the topic gets short shrift in a section that mentions that, oh, by the way, good writing is a fundamental part of any ideas-based business and you need to do a lot of it, including write a good book.

In fact, most books on thought leadership leave the reader high and dry about how to write well.

Here I will show you how to find and write those stories that reflect your purpose, unique viewpoint and expertise to position you as an authority in your niche.

Let's get started.

PART ONE

FIND YOUR THOUGHT-LEADERSHIP NICHE

CHAPTER **1**

Thought Leadership, Writing and Ideas

"Thought leaders are, at their core, meaning makers" —Matt Church

As a professional writer and editor, I am frequently asked to work on articles written by teams of subject-matter experts about their business.

I'm talking about 800-1,500-word pieces meant to go into a magazine or blog and designed to show the fresh thinking of the writers and their organization. The stories are meant to serve as conversation starters with the expert's clients and prospects.

Over the years, I must have edited thousands of these pieces about topics like supply chain, agile project management or some detail about accounting or finance.

Many of the stories I worked on were chock full of really good ideas.

There was only one problem.

By the time I discovered the interesting ideas in the story, I was falling asleep.

Or I had at least considered a nap.

The next step was to go on a call with the team of experts-cum-writers to get their buy-in for an edit that would be deeper than expected. I found myself having hundreds of conversations with really smart and accomplished people about what could be improved in their articles.

Usually, the conversations went something like this: I would refer to paragraphs at the top of the text, usually where they were setting up the problem, and say, "The reader knows this, we've heard that, yep, we know that bit, too."

... by getting your story framed correctly from the beginning, you can greatly improve your writing for your business.

Then, as we progressed toward the end, usually at the bottom quarter of the story, I'd say, "Aha! That's interesting. That's new. That's exciting. That's your story! Why don't we kick out the stuff at the top, move this interesting material forward and build that out as the story?"

I now call these types of conversations with experts "story-framing" sessions.

After leading hundreds, if not thousands, of story-framing sessions, I began to ask myself: What am I actually doing in these calls? What was I showing and teaching and explaining?

How was I able to convince the experts that their hard work of writing had resulted in a dull article, but that they could make it very interesting by getting the story angle right?

To find out what I was doing, I had to deconstruct my own process. In doing so, I discovered one of my main ideas: By getting your story framed correctly from the beginning, you can greatly improve your writing for your business.

This is a little-known truth: Story framing is one of the most important parts of good writing, but it's one of the most often overlooked. If story framing isn't currently part of your content-creation process, don't blame yourself. Frankly, it is also under-taught.

Help yourself be heard

How many times have you launched on creating a piece of content but been unclear what the message is, what's new about it, or how it will bring the conversation forward? Or how many times have you watched companies do this? You simply want to shout out: Get to the point!

I have encountered so many experts who love to write and who long to get out into the world and be heard.

But too often, these experts are too smart for their own good, and their writing sounds like it's straight from academia (code word: hard to read).

For the sake of innovation, and to make this world a better place to live, we need to hear your authentic message. And that message needs to break through in an arena where the non-experts are the ones currently hogging the microphone.

The fight against industrialized content has begun

Another core idea of this book is that the modern content creation model is broken and moving in the wrong direction. It needs to be disintermediated.

How do I disintermediate the world's broken content model?

By enabling you—the subject matter expert—to have narrative instincts and story smarts.

When experts can find and frame their best ideas to make them accessible to a wider audience, there's more possibility to solve the big problems in this world. There's also more room for new ideas for products, services and solutions. Of course, this also means there is less need for content intermediaries like marketing specialists, communications gurus, ghostwriters, and the like.

These content intermediaries do important work, but they may not know all there is to know about a given subject. They will not be privy to as many ideas and the types of ideas that people in the business can have because intermediaries aren't exposed to the same environment.

This leads us back to the importance of experts framing their own stories. Once they have a great story, marketing can enhance and improve on it from there, selling the heck out of it.

Marketing and PR teams are always keen on innovative ideas. But if those innovative ideas aren't properly brought forward to them, they might not have a lot to work with.

That's why I say innovation, disruption and the best ideas are most likely already living in the heads of people like you—the experts who are running the business, doing the research and talking to clients every day.

When experts are enabled with story smarts, they start making their ideas real and tangible on a daily basis, thereby boosting the business, bringing research forward and infusing creativity into their work.

Hearing your authentic voice out there in the world is just the antidote we need to the canned content that spams us from left and right every day.

Innovation, disruption and the best ideas are most likely already living in the heads of people like you—the experts who are running businesses, doing research and talking to clients every day.

It is our responsibility as experts on a journey to thought leadership to contribute uniquely and authentically to the bigger conversation. It's not only good for you and your career prospects, it's also good for your organization and your clients.

Content looking for an author

Here's an example: I had a client in marketing who pre-ordered blog posts from an agency for the experts in his firm. Journalists ghostwrote the stories, so they were decent. But then he had to shop around inside the firm to find an expert he could assign the content to.

Yep, that's right.

The marketing guy needed to find the expert who would allegedly write the story *after* it was already ghostwritten.

If that isn't backward and canned content, I don't know what is.

My goal here is to help you get your unique and useful ideas out into the world in a way that makes them accessible.

This is the antithesis of canned content.

What's in it for me?

Why is this so important to me?

I want to see progress, hope and light. I know that we already have what we need to solve our biggest problems. We have the solutions, but many of the ideas aren't being heard because they're stuck inside an expert's head, buried in a text or otherwise inaccessible.

If you're among those experts who have a burning need to share your ideas—ideas that matter—but you're struggling to get your ideas heard, then you're in the right place.

Sometimes it happens like this: You know you're on to something good. You can feel it. You've been mulling your ideas. Maybe you've written them down, created a scribble, developed a workshop or held a presentation around some of your thinking. From talking to people and

19

reading and writing, you know that your thoughts about your niche subject are something your audience needs and craves.

But how will you reach your audience on a wide scale? There are so many voices out there. They're loud.

In my opinion, there's only one reliable way to stand out.

You've got to approach the story in the right way and tell it like a journalist would: You need to write like a thought leader.

Ideas and their inherent value

The question I'd like to begin with is what makes an idea good?

Someone asked me just that in a call when I was reviewing his work. After that conversation, I thought about it more and began to shape what had come out as my spontaneous answer. Thanks to his question, I came up with this new piece of intellectual property. (See Figure 2.)

Five qualities of a good idea

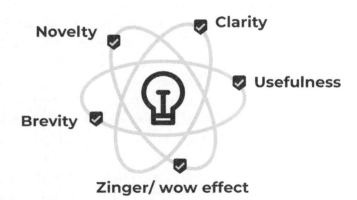

Figure 2—Five qualities of a good idea

Judging ideas is something that I have been doing for a long time as a writer and editor. First, I look for an idea to be **novel**. Is it new, different, unusual? Have I heard it put that way before?

Second, I believe ideas must be **useful**. Grand as an idea may be, if it's not useful for your audience then it won't gain traction.

Third, I want ideas to be served up to me **clearly**. Make sure I get it, and make sure I get it fast. If that's not happening, then your idea may not be articulated as well as it should be.

Fourth, keep it **short**, sweetheart.

Fifth and finally, give me a dose of dopamine when I hear your idea for the first time. Good ideas come with a **wow effect**. They make you anticipate a reward. They're like a zinger. Or it feels like you've been bit by a good idea that wants to use you as its host.

Defining thought leadership

Ideas are what thought leaders traffic in. Consider these people concept peddlers, if you will.

How do I define thought leaders?

Thought leaders are people on the forefront of the ideas in their niche. They are the ones who are identifying trends and naming the things that are happening in a field that remain as-yet unnamed.

Typically, thought leaders are ideas-driven people with an urge to share their ideas and a language for doing so that makes those ideas accessible. Thought leaders simplify the complex, connect dots and steer the agenda in their area.

Thought leadership is a term that has reached buzzword status and, as happens with buzzwords, it has gotten over-used. Companies may promote their thought-leadership campaigns when, in fact, these are nothing but standard marketing campaigns based on salesy materials.

If everyone is a thought leader, then no one is a thought leader.

Similarly, if you find someone who is calling themself a thought leader, proceed with caution. I haven't come across too many people who seem to have anointed themselves this way, but I'm sure it has happened. In my view, the term "thought leader" can and should be protected and bestowed on others carefully. It is not something to be given by you to yourself.

Why's that?

If everyone is a thought leader, then no one is a thought leader.

In my workshops, I have discovered that some people struggle with defining the term thought leader. One way I explain a thought leader is to compare the term to the more common market leader: Market leaders are ahead in the race to sell products or services, while **thought leaders are those individuals and companies who are ahead in the race to establish ideas.**

In general, I see thought leaders as subject-matter experts who:

- Give useful advice from a fresh perspective
- Publish widely
- Influence their field
- Steer the conversation
- Set the agenda

Instead of waiting to see the shape of the future, thought leaders actively mold it by articulating what is new, different and important, and they do so in a way that is engaging. In short, thought leaders are sought after for the clarity and originality of their ideas. Often, they have a knack for simplifying the complex and turning complex ideas into compelling stories.

Mark Levy, the author of "Accidental Genius: Using Writing to Generate Your Best Ideas, Insight and Content," defines the job of a thought leader as being a provocateur.

Send up your flare

Many people go about their daily work too focused, with their heads down, he says. "As a thought leader, you come up with an idea and you send it out there, and it's like a flare. People with their heads down see the light reflecting off their desk, and they kind of have to look up to say, 'What was that?'"

People consider the flare that you've sent up, and they can incorporate it into their lives—or not. But at least you've helped them raise their sights temporarily and think in a different way, Levy said.

What business leaders want in thought-leadership writing

According to the B2B thought leadership agency Grist, 66% of senior executives use thought leadership materials to stay ahead of emerging trends, and 60% consume it to help them make more informed decisions. This data is from a survey Grist conducted a few years back of more than 200 executives at FTSE 350 companies[*]. I believe it is still relevant for the topic at hand.

---

[*] See regular "Value of B2B thought leadership" surveys by Grist at gristonline.com.

Grist found executives were looking for articles far more often than they wanted white papers, videos or podcasts. The survey showed senior executives preferred:

- **Short articles** of 800 words—63%
- **Blog posts** of 300–500 words—57%
- **Feature articles** of 1,200+ words—45%

What did the executives want in those articles?

- **Fresh thinking**: Exploring issues or challenges from new and different perspectives—46%
- **Forward-thinking**: Analyzing important or emerging trends—32%
- **Evidence-led**: Containing robust data—29%
- **Action-oriented**: Including recommendations that help you make more informed decisions—26%
- **Authentic**: Originating from existing expertise—26%

Knowing what readers want is the first step. Executing thought-leadership content in high quality at a program level is a different matter.

In its 2020 Thought Leadership Impact Study, Edelman, the global communications firm, said, B2B buyers were getting harder to impress and were disappointed with the content some brands were giving them.

Only 32% of decision-makers that year said they reliably gained valuable insights from consuming thought leadership—down from 39% in 2018. And more decision-makers (29%) believed that most of what they consume was "mediocre to very poor" in terms of quality (compared to 26% in 2018), Edelman wrote.

However, on the bright side, Edelman said decision-makers affirmed that when done well, thought leadership content positively influences their own purchasing behaviors.

In general, there are five broad phases in the journey from subject-matter expert to thought leader. (See Figure 3.)

The journey from subject-matter expert to thought leader

1 – Curiosity
You're excited by a set of ideas and begin to explore them

2 – Study
You go deep in this area and consume all you can

3 – Mastery
You become a master of your area of study or work

4 – Externalization
You learn to articulate your ideas and make them accessible to a wider audience

5 – Delivery as a thought leader
You deliver your ideas regularly to a wide audience and begin building a community around them and your goals for the greater good

Figure 3—The journey from subject-matter expert to thought leader

It all begins with **curiosity** about a subject or idea. You're intrigued. You want to learn more. You spend all your extra time or, if you're lucky, much of your work time, exploring the idea or ideas that have bit you.

Maybe this is a curiosity you've harbored since childhood. Author Malcolm Gladwell was fascinated with tipping points since he was a boy, long before writing his bestselling book about them.

The second phase is **study** of the idea or idea set. You collect, you read, you question, you interview. You're fascinated and must learn more.

Then comes **mastery**. That involves lots of time, dedication, stops, starts, wins and failures. You're so convinced your idea is valuable that you keep going, sometimes without considering the costs.

In the fourth phase, **externalization**, you're going out to the world with your ideas. Here's where your story smarts will come in handy. An idea is just a piece of nebulous matter if it's stuck in your head. You must articulate it for it to become tangible and shareable.

It's best to articulate your idea with a narrative kernel that makes your idea relevant and memorable for a wider audience.

The fifth phase is **delivery** as a thought leader, which also requires you to draw on your narrative skills. In this phase, you build a community around your ideas and your goals for the greater good.

Thought leaders and content marketing

Whether you're independent or work for a company, you need to do so-called content marketing to get your ideas heard, and that content should be less about the marketing and more about the ideas. In other words, your marketing efforts should be based on the thought-leadership materials you create.

Although I deplore the term content marketing, the idea is smart because once you've invested in good writing, or created multimedia with the right storyline, your content can continue to live on and generate lead after lead for your business. You can scale your audience and your revenues around your good content, without always having to create something new over and over again.

But if your content isn't of high quality—if you're writing is stale and convoluted—you won't attract any interest or start any conversations. Your whole content marketing strategy will collapse.

In a world of oversupply, Google rightly rewards higher-quality content. By producing it, you can reap the benefit over the long term. There is no additional cost to you if your content attracts 20 viewers or 200,000.

That means there's no additional cost to you if 200,000 people happen to see your offering that is alongside—but not part of—your content.

What is this elusive good content people keep talking about?

It is strong conceptual, ideas-driven work, whether that is in the form of thought-leadership writing or multimedia materials.

And what makes strong conceptual, ideas-driven work?

It's based on fresh and compelling ideas that articulate a truth about a subject matter that many people have pondered or felt, but few have named or unpacked.

Key takeaways

- Thought leaders are those people who are ahead in the race to establish ideas.
- They shape the conversation and the agenda in their niche with fresh perspectives and compelling stories.
- As content becomes more industrialized, it is unique ideas that will make your content stand out.
- To find more unique ideas, it is important to understand the anatomy of a good idea.
- As you move along the journey from subject-matter expert to thought leader, having story smarts will become increasingly important.

CHAPTER 2

What Is
Thought-Leadership Writing?

"HARD WRITING MAKES EASY READING. EASY WRITING
MAKES HARD READING" —WILLIAM ZINSSER

Now let's look at writing in the thought-leadership style. Thought-leadership writing is writing that explores solutions to a problem that plagues your audience. It is born of your thought-leadership niche and brings in your opinion and life or work experience.

Ideally, it will extract lessons learned and serve them up in a usable way for readers. It provides all this value while explicitly avoiding salesy or marketing language. Instead, thought-leadership writing has an associated, but separate, commercial offering.

This type of writing shows the breadth and depth of your experience. In magazine, feature-length pieces, it is about subjects you research and study. For example, it is the highlights from that research or the research itself.

In newspaper or web-length stories, thought-leadership writing reflects the knowledge you have gained from your own client, project or personal experience.

Thought-leadership writing is writing that explores solutions to a problem that plagues your audience. It is born of your thought-leadership niche and brings in your opinion and life or work experience.

Often, people with a knowledge-based product or service to sell write thought-leadership materials to demonstrate their mastery of a subject, or their fresh thinking about it.

The purpose of the articles is to get the writer's name or company name associated with that body of knowledge—and a unique view on that knowledge.

Commercial intent through an altruistic approach

Thought-leadership writing has a commercial intent, but it doesn't have a salesy tone or character.

Instead, it is based on a good-natured effort to lead your reader to new understanding and share ideas that may be helpful. By doing so, the author has the chance to earn the trust of their audience.

It's important to remember that to write like a thought leader, you must give away your knowledge for free, with no strings attached. It is disingenuous to slip in a salesy message to this style of writing, or to present a solution and then mention that you happen to provide that solution for a handsome fee.

Ideally, it will extract lessons learned and serve them up in a usable way for readers. It provides all this value while explicitly avoiding salesy or marketing language. Instead, thought-leadership writing has an associated, but separate, commercial offering.

By doing so, you risk spoiling your piece and annoying your audience with covert advertising. Be warned: Do it too often and your audience will learn to click away fast.

In "Writing Down the Bones: Freeing the Writer Within," Natalie Goldberg says that writers don't need to lock up their best ideas and hold them back. Instead, we need to trust in ourselves that our great ideas can be put forth into the world and then, after they've been released, we'll just have more great ideas.

Cannibalizing your own business?

Understandably, some people worry that if they give away too much of their "secret sauce" they will cannibalize their own business. They think that a potential client won't hire them because that client has already learned the expert's best practices through a piece of writing. Similarly, scientists may worry that fellow researchers or peers may steal their ideas.

Writing like a thought leader in short form writing is different because there's little chance that you'll give away too much. Often, what you're selling is the implementation of an idea that people cannot perform without you. You will not lose potential business by sharing your helpful ideas. On the contrary, you're doing a valuable service to your reader that is likely to boost your business.

Sometimes when I tell people that I'm a former journalist now working for companies, they assume that I write advertising copy. I explain that I am using my journalistic skills in the service of companies, but I'm not writing ads, nor am I writing salesy-sounding texts. Yes, the stories I edit and ghostwrite are used to market a company's product or services, but they do it in a subtle way, and they do it subtly by design. I call this the "by the way" approach to marketing. In other words, the texts implicitly say, "Hey, by the way, we offer this or that related service."

Thought leaders are ideas guides

The by-the-way marketing effect happens after a reader has learned something in your story, been made curious by a new perspective, or has experienced a complex problem made easier to understand. The reader becomes downright grateful.

Think about it. The knowledge held by humans is expanding so rapidly that no one can possibly keep up. To be given applied knowledge, or to come across collected wisdom or best practices is refreshing, and the person who gave us that will gain the trust of readers and be rewarded.

Rewards come when readers share the information or become a client. It's the law of attraction. Well-executed articles make you attractive to those who need what you have to offer, and that's a valuable position to be in. It's much better than if you just cranked out another marketing promotion.

In a short-form article, there's little chance that you'll give away so much that the reader can solve the problem alone.

Despite these compelling arguments, people still balk at giving away knowledge for free.

Sometimes I have thought about jokingly asking people in my workshops to stand and repeat after me, holding their right hand in the air, as if taking an oath: "I solemnly swear to give away my knowledge for free, no strings attached."

This is one of the most difficult things for people new to the genre to accept. I work with lots of consultants and hear repeatedly why they cannot tell this or that point about their 3-step methodology or the 5-step plan, or whatever is the basis of the solution they're writing about.

I explain why it's necessary to do so: If the story is going to be about solving an urgent problem, which is often the case for consultants, you've got to talk about the solution in depth and show a fresh perspective. In a short-form article, there's little chance that you'll give away so much that the reader can solve the problem alone.

In the case of consultants, they are selling multi-million-dollar projects with specialized skills and knowledge. They have benchmark data and best practices collected from across clients and projects, but they may resist writing articles with depth.

As a result, the company appears to only scrape the surface, doesn't give readers what they need, and risks losing the reader forever.

Thought-leadership writing = Simple writing

An article written in the thought-leadership style doesn't need to be complicated to make a strong point. Consider a piece by the financial analyst and forensic economist Stephen Horan that got more than 48,000 views on Forbes. It was called "Four Ways to Save More of Your Paycheck." Horan is a former managing director at CFA Institute, the global association for investment professionals.

Now why would someone as smart as Horan—who has a doctorate, is a Chartered Financial Analyst, and has a host of other certifications—want to create an article about saving more of your paycheck, and why did this story get so much attention?

Because among his other work, Horan had an interest in making sure that investment professionals have clients to serve in the years to come.

He's addressing a pressing problem that's facing nearly every person in this world, which is saving more of our paychecks. If people don't save, then soon enough there won't be any need for investment professionals. He has looked at the pipeline of future investors and understood what may keep them from investing in years to come. For these reasons, Horan got out there, talked about his own experience and concerns, and provided ideas for how to manage our own behavior to save more. His article had traction.

All this is to say that even if the article's approach appears simplistic, it can still be part of a body of work that adds up to thought leadership for a person or an institution.

Thought leadership in short-form work

As mentioned, thought-leadership stories have a commercial intent, minus the advertising language. The moment that a story veers toward advertising or copywriting, it is no longer thought-leadership writing. That's the number one knockout criteria. But where do you draw the line on what constitutes thought-leadership writing?

What I am saying is that in working to meet the style requirements of this type of writing, you can quickly improve your writing for your own business, career or company.

Here's where I draw it: As long as it's not salesy, if an individual piece of your work meets *some* of the basic criteria of thought-leadership materials, it is valuable. I am not saying every piece of writing is going to check every box to be a top-notch story in the thought-leadership style. What I am saying is that in working to meet the style requirements of this type of writing, you can quickly improve your writing for your own business, career or company.

Two of the most important criteria are a) that your stories be solutions focused and b) that they give away your knowledge without asking anything in return. But there are many more characteristics, a few of which I've mapped out below. (See Figure 4.)

Characteristics of effective, short-form writing in the thought-leadership style

Figure 4—Characteristics of effective, short-form writing in the thought-leadership style

Let's look at the mind map in more detail here as a list. Effective thought-leadership writing:

- Says why the idea is important
  - It addresses:
    - What's at stake?
    - Why now?
    - What if something doesn't happen?
    - What if something does happen?

- Says why you care
  - May include personal-interest stories
  - Tells what you want in the form of a call to action
  - Considers how you want your audience to feel

- Is conversational
  - It:
    - Is quotable (Where are your soundbites?)
    - Is written like you talk
    - Includes short sentences
    - States complex ideas succinctly

- Is structured
  - It:
    - Has a beginning, a middle and an end
    - Tells what you're planning to focus on (e.g., includes a journalistic nut graf)
    - Wraps up main points at the end

- Has a fresh angle on common subjects
  - An idea applied
  - An idea expanded

- Shows your humanity
  - Shows humility
  - Shows you are vulnerable
  - Imparts knowledge and best practices

- Uses rhetorical devices
  - Repetition

- Triads
- Metaphor

- Is based on your experience
  - Imparts learned and earned wisdom

- Is strategic
  - Lays out the pros and cons of options
  - Solves a problem

- Is not salesy
  - Your offering is separated from the story

Easy enough? Yeah right.

Don't worry. I'm going to walk you through the way journalists do it.

The world needs your unique perspective

Ideally, thought-leadership writing is writing about solutions that you care about deeply, since you have been there and want to spare others the pain you went through.

Maybe, for example, you know a lot about project management and how to roll out software. You know because you've done it many, many times, and learned from mistakes.

This experience will give you a unique perspective for writing about the problems that are a part of software rollouts.

Or perhaps you're a financial advisor focused on clients who have just received a windfall payment. You know that without the right psychological and emotional support, people who have won lotteries, been paid out large amounts from lawsuits, or inherited wealth may squander their funds within a few years or a single generation.

Thought-leadership writing is essentially service writing because you aim to help your reader by taking over some bit of the thinking, research or articulation related to the problem you are addressing.

Maybe you are a coach who has seen other coaches hijack a project, and you have some thoughts on why they are behaving this way, and what can be done about it.

If you are writing thought-leadership materials for your own business or career goals, the aim is to focus on solutions that you know have worked and which can potentially help others.

Thought-leadership writing = Service writing

In journalism, we have a category called service journalism.

It's all about presenting useful and vetted information to readers so they can make better choices, for instance on preparing their homes for winter, selecting a college or choosing a financial advisor.

Thought-leadership writing is essentially *service* writing because you aim to help your reader by taking over some bit of the thinking, research or articulation related to the problem you are addressing.

That's the service part.

You're helping the reader because you have experienced something that you now want to share about. Maybe it was a project, a process, or a burnout you lived to tell about. Whatever it is, you've done a great deal of thinking about and/or researching the subject matter and are now serving the reader by sharing that.

Thought leadership writing = Solutions writing

In journalism, we also have something called solutions journalism[*].

I say thought-leadership writing isn't only service writing, it's also *solutions* writing because you come at the reader with concrete ideas about how to approach a particular problem in a better way.

The source of the solutions you present may be from your own experience or your research. They may be your own ideas or the application of the ideas of others in a way that is uniquely yours.

Solutions can be large or small, tangible or intangible. They may be about how to live a more fulfilling life by conquering so-called "imposter" syndrome, or how to perform a particular business process better, such as vetting your suppliers.

The passion and purpose imperative

That said, if your writing is only about providing a service to the reader or explaining a solution, that's probably not enough to make it fall in the thought-leadership category.

To do that, the ideas you write about need to resonate with your passion and purpose, and the prose needs to be written in a way that is accessible.

Let's say you're a consultant who wants to share ideas on LinkedIn about how to speed up

The source of the solutions you present may be from your own experience or your research. They may be your own ideas or the application of the ideas of others in a way that is uniquely yours.

---

[*] Search online for the Solutions Journalism Network to learn more.

the product development cycle at large consumer-goods companies whose territory is being encroached on by startups.

That's valuable thinking about solutions that can be very helpful for such companies. But if there is no deeper connection between the writer and the subject matter, or the story is written in an academic fashion, it may fall flat.

By developing and then explaining the big ideas you have, why they're important and why they're important to you, you tantalize the reader to want to know more.

You gain the readers' trust with writing that illustrates deep expertise and creativity, and readers may very well reward you by seeking out your commercial offering.

Thought-leadership writing uses the "push" effect

To use the language of consultants, advertising copy is meant to have a "pull" effect. It entices readers toward a product or service.

Thought-leadership writing, however, is meant to have a "push" effect because the author is providing the reader with their knowledge about a solution. They are "pushing" their knowledge into the world and pointing it in the reader's direction, which is much more altruistic and far less manipulative than the way advertising works.

In his book "Give and Take: Why Helping Others Drives Our Success," management expert Adam Grant argues that givers have the most success in work and life because their generosity is rewarded. Thought leaders seem to have inherently understood Grant's idea: They instinctively give away their knowledge for free.

Whether you are writing a book, a paper or an article, thought-leadership writing serves your reader by simplifying the complex, applying thinking from one field to another, or offering creative solutions where they are desperately needed.

It can be about trends in global finance, putting artificial intelligence to use, social or workplace problems, or, as organizing ace Marie Kondo has shown, getting control of your closet.

Your subject matter doesn't matter that much, so long as you're passionate about it, meeting a need, and enriching the discussion with a fresh perspective.

Key takeaways

- Thought-leadership writing is solutions writing with an opinion and an underlying—but separate—commercial offering.
- If you describe your offering as an offering, or sell in your story, then it is not thought-leadership writing.
- This type of writing gives away your knowledge or your company's knowledge for free.
- In return, individuals and companies raise their own standing in the reader's eyes and win trust.
- Done well, short-form articles can form a body of work that distinguishes you as a thought leader or associates your name with expertise in a particular area.

CHAPTER 3

Becoming an Ideas Machine

"EVERY ACT OF PERCEPTION IS AN ATTEMPT
TO IMPOSE ORDER, TO MAKE SENSE OF A
CHAOTIC UNIVERSE" —JOHN YORKE

To write in the thought-leadership style, you need quality, core ideas and new, interesting angles for telling stories that present you as an authority in your niche.

On your journey to thought leadership, one main goal is for you to become a walking, talking ideas machine who uses your ideas in the service of your audience.

You've got to have a steady stream of your own great ideas to write about, and you need to build a community around your ideas so that they have an impact on a broad scale.

When you have honed your ideation skills, you'll readily have the next idea already on tap. You'll know how to observe something and spin it forward to articulate a trend that others are just beginning to sense. This is a skill you can learn.

On your journey to thought leadership, one main goal is for you to become a walking, talking ideas machine who uses your ideas in the service of your audience.

What, you ask, is an ideator?

An ideator is a person who can capture intuition, hunches and ideas and hold this nebulous matter in their mind long enough to develop it further and give the idea expression through language.

If an idea is unexpressed by its originator, then it never existed. It cannot be applied or transformed by someone else until it is expressed. Many experts have great ideas that get stuck in their heads simply because they lack the tools to externalize them by articulating them and giving them a narrative kernel.

Data vs. ideas

Some people like to say that data is the new oil.

I think that as our economies and societies become ever more knowledge-based, *ideas* are the new oil, not data. Ideas are valuable because they help us self-actualize in our private lives, relationships and work. And that self-actualization is central to being human.

An ideator is a person who can capture intuition, hunches and ideas and hold this nebulous matter in their mind long enough to develop it further and give the idea expression through language.

On the job, you are judged daily by *how* you do your work. That's what performance reviews are all about. But over the long run, you'll be remembered for the ideas you bring to your work.

Why?

Because it is your ideas that make you unique. It is your ideas that make you memorable. That is assuming you've put them into a linguistic form that makes your ideas understandable and applicable.

Similarly, it is ideas that are most valuable for us to move ahead as a society. Think about how long it took for some of the world's biggest ideas to make it from the germ stage to the new normal—the combustion engine, human flight, the internet.

We were born to have ideas

Having and articulating ideas is also good for your health. Consider the joy that comes with coming up with something novel. This joy is a positive—and healthy—side effect of maintaining an ideas habit.

As humans, one of the greatest satisfactions in life is creative production. What you produce creatively doesn't really matter. It can be new ideas or tweaked ideas in the form of books, art, poetry, theater, recipes, construction, handicrafts, products, services or processes. The point is that you see your ideas come to fruition.

I strongly believe that when life throws you a curve ball, when you're suffering hardships and aren't sure how to continue, you can sustain yourself with creative productivity. You can create meaning in the face of adversity by cultivating and feeding an ideas habit.

I think that many people understand this intuitively.

By launching our ideas into the world, we can pay forward our creative energy and the solutions we have for the problems we face. Who knows how they will be built upon years, decades, or even centuries after we have departed?

Articulating the value you bring

On a project I worked on recently, I overheard partners at a big IT consulting firm talking about how important it is to articulate value to their existing clients.

One partner had called together a team of consultants who were given the job of making a list of ways that their company had provided value for the client. This is a language-based task, but it was the subject-matter experts in the business who were asked to collect the ideas with little or no training in articulation, ideation or writing.

It struck me as a bit unfair and difficult for engineers and other specialists to be given that task. That's when I began to think about value articulation as a process.

How would I break it down to explain it to the engineers? I came up with what you see in Figure 5: How to articulate what is as-yet unarticulated.

How to articulate what is as-yet unarticulated

Steps:

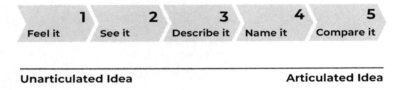

Figure 5—How to articulate what is as-yet unarticulated

Step 1: Feel it

An idea usually emerges as a feeling that comes after long inquiry into a subject. First you are intrigued and curious and start investigating. Then you can feel if the idea is close or still far away from being put into words. It's still unspoken in this phase, but it's taking form as a sense, an intuition or a hunch.

Step 2: See it

As the idea is incubating in your mind, you notice more proof points to back it up. Your keen observation skills are at work to solidify your emerging opinion. As you focus energy in that direction, you begin to see signs that show that what you're talking about does or can exist in the physical or mental realm.

Step 3: Describe it

Because you can feel it and are starting to see this fuzzy thing take shape, you search for language to describe it. You can talk around it and attribute characteristics to this idea, and the more you describe the idea, the more it takes form. Here freewriting, list making, mind mapping, chartifying, or even getting interviewed by someone can help. (More on these in Chapter 5.)

Step 4: Name it

Next, you begin trying out names for the concept. Is it this, or is it that? Which name is the truer or closer one that conveys the concept concisely and precisely? What is the idea in three to five words? In this step, you make attempts at naming the idea. You give the concept a "working title" if you will.

Step 5: Compare it

To make the idea relatable and to give it the necessary context, the next step is to compare it to something. What is it like or how does it seem? Where have you seen something similar before? By comparing the idea and describing it with a metaphor (or something close to a metaphor), you bestow the idea with the status of having been both articulated and put into context

Turning hunches into stories

The process I describe above is like one taught to report-ers, particularly investigative reporters. They are taught to become aware of and be able to articulate their hunches. Those hunches are based on observations, intuition and empathy. The reporter has become skilled in presuppos-ing what might be going on in a situation or what might be buried beneath the surface.

Once a hunch becomes more concrete, then they can begin the chase and the process of backing up their hunch. Similarly, you may have intuition about a given idea in your niche that is not yet well-articulated, or you may be able to sense the default assumptions at play and begin to give them form with words.

As Vikram Mansharamani, the author of "Think For Yourself" says, "in an age of experts and artificial intelli-gence, depth of expertise must be balanced with breadth of perspective."

Well-shaped and well-shared ideas distinguish thought leaders from experts

I believe we need plenty of experts and plenty of people striving for thought leadership, as well as a few actual thought leaders who serve as guiding lights.

Some people will surely not be up for the risk that comes with full-on thought leadership, such as the criti-cism you will face and the ideas you attempt to bring to life that will, on occasion, fail to gain traction, even if they're well-articulated.

And that's fine. There's a place for everyone who is interested in trafficking in ideas and creating stories that benefit your audience.

One main difference between experts and thought leaders is their level of story smarts, which include skills of the spoken word, the written word and concept development. Emerging thought leaders know how to capture their thinking, articulate it and make it relevant for their audiences in articles that have dramatic tension.

Dramatic tension is what makes the reader want to proceed. In fiction, it's the material that keeps the reader asking, "What happens next?" In nonfiction, dramatic tension can come in the form of a promised pay-off or transformation you'll help the reader go through.

Usually in three phases, you will have hooked the reader, sustained their interest by delivering on the promise you made, and wrapped it up at the end.

Adam Grant, a professor and author of "Give and Take: Why Helping Others Drives Our Success," "Originals," and many other works, has a way of doing this in his writing.

He is a thought leader in organizational psychology and has fine-tuned story smarts. I asked Grant about his process for finding ideas and stories. He said he begins with evidence from social science and then looks for ways to illustrate it.

Grant said he:

- Identifies some fields that go to the extreme on the characteristics or skills in question

- Reaches out to people who have written or spoken about the phenomenon

- Looks for people who have won awards or been recognized for the quality

- Contacts people who live the principles or know the subject matter, and asks who they admire

- Picks something he loves and starts digging to see who was behind it
- Pays attention in everyday life

Below, I have examined the differences between subject-matter experts and thought leaders, mostly related to the story smarts that are needed for thought leadership. (See Figure 6.)

Differences between subject-matter experts and thought leaders

TYPE OF SKILL/AREA	SUBJECT-MATTER EXPERTS	THOUGHT LEADERS/ EMERGING THOUGHT LEADERS
Cognitive	Smart and usually educated	Smart and usually educated, but don't necessarily have to be trained in a classical sense
	Focused on a niche with an understanding of the big picture	Focused on a niche with an exceptional understanding of the big picture, including the picture outside of the field
Community orientation	Know a lot but have no strong need to share that knowledge. Just finding out and knowing what they know is often gratifying enough.	Know a lot and want to share it with the world
	Are not particularly concerned with building and leading a community	Are concerned with building and leading a community of people who want to make a certain change
Visibility	Somewhat invisible in his/her/ their expertise	A visible expert
Spoken word	Speak in jargon and have trouble translating what they do for general audiences	Speak in plain language and can explain what they do quickly and easily in the form of memorable stories
Written word	Write in an inaccessible way/ academic way	Use the journalistic skill set for their writing, sometimes in combination with a base of academic materials. Thought leaders have an ability to tease out the most salient details for the audience and serve them up nicely as stories. They are able to put their work into context and spin ideas forward.

TYPE OF SKILL/AREA	SUBJECT-MATTER EXPERTS	THOUGHT LEADERS/ EMERGING THOUGHT LEADERS
Concept development	Concept-aware Subject-matter experts identify strong concepts when they see them. In some cases, they may be overly focused on the explicit.	Concept-driven Thought leaders articulate strong concepts as they emerge. They focus on the implicit as well as the explicit.
Ideation	Know a well-codified idea when they see one	Are able to deconstruct their own processes and ideas to codify them so they are accessible to others. Similarly, they are able to see and articulate the guiding principles at play in their own work and in that of others.
	Focus on knowledge	Focus on knowledge and ideas
Trend-spotting	Play an important part in trends, but may not necessarily understand their role fully	Play an important part in trends, and see their role as identifying, understanding and shaping those trends as they emerge

Figure 6—Differences between subject-matter experts and thought leaders

The creative process

For emerging thought leaders, part of the creative process will also include creating your own intellectual property.

That may sound high and mighty. You may be daunted, or perhaps you feel that's all a bit pompous. Who, me? Create my own intellectual property?

That's right. Most everyone can create their own intellectual property if they're of a mind to do so. When my first pieces popped out, I was surprised and delighted. I generated them by doing writing and conceptual exercises from prompts I had found in my research on thought leadership.

That's how I came up with 5 Ps that describe the writing process. They were messy at first. Here's a cleaned-up version.

Five steps to the writing process:

Step 1: **Peruse** ideas (prepare your idea and material)

Step 2: **Pluck** ideas (conduct interviews and collect select background information/research)

Step 3: **Prune** your material (reduce your material and narrow your focus)

Step 4: **Put** and **play** (write, and have fun with it; in German, *schriftsteller* **translates as someone who places words, or a "word-'put-er'"**)

Step 5: **Polish** your text (rewrite)

At first, this book was going to be structured around the 5 P's I created, but as my ideas began to gel, I realized that this is not the essence of what I want to be speaking to people about.

It's important to see writing as a process, and I was tickled that I could get everything into P form, but this was not the real matter at hand. For that reason, I kicked it out as a core idea after having asked myself, "Do I want to be interviewed about the 5 P's on somebody's show?"

My answer was no. So, out it went. I bring it up here to show the Ps as an example of intellectual property.

How can you generate ideas about your subject in this fashion?

I started with list-making, freewriting and sketching ideas in a spiral, lined notebook.

If imposter syndrome is rearing its head for you right now because I have suggested you create your own intellectual property, let it be. I believe this is the best way to handle it: Don't start an argument with the judge in your head who is mocking you and questioning your abilities. Just acknowledge him but refuse to engage.

I like to use a phrase I once heard in the context of the judge: "So you say." Tell the judge in your head who is saying you cannot do it, or any other person who might be trying to define you externally, "so you say."

If you want to create your own intellectual property, you can. If someone, including your judge, says you can't, the answer is: "So you say."

Ideas are one big conversation, and if you are conversing, which I assume you are, then you have your own unique viewpoint on what you're hearing, and, obviously, what you're saying. You have an opinion about what is right and wrong, good and bad, on-spot or off-target.

> *Don't start an argument with the judge in your head who is mocking you and questioning your abilities. Just acknowledge him but refuse to engage.*

The goal is to get those ideas out of your head and into the world in spoken or written form. After that, you can turn them into something visual, such as a figure.

A descent into chaos

As you move forward in the process, it can feel like a bumpy ride. The act of conceptualization requires a descent into chaos. You've got to visit a realm where messiness and fuzziness prevail and filter what you see through your own experience to unearth something valuable to others.

As an emerging thought leader, you're a problem-solver and guide for your audience. That means you've got to descend where others may be reluctant to go.

You've got to unpack cognitive dissonance, bias and assumptions around the problems you are solving and examine them in new ways. This may feel uncomfortable for a while, but when you re-emerge with a clear idea that is well-articulated and valuable to your audience, you will be rewarded and feel great.

Deconstruct your own process

One way to generate new intellectual property is to deconstruct your own process.

This means: Start noticing what you do (your processes) and how you do it (your how).

Make a list of all the processes you do within your niche. Begin taking notes. Begin lining up steps and points on a blank piece of paper. This is the back-of-the napkin work.

Did you just explain something to someone about your area of interest? Grab a sheet and write down what you said in bullets, step by step.

Or grab a blank PowerPoint with all its template figures, such as triangles, matrices, lists and funnels. Then start plugging in your ideas. The more freewriting, list-making and mind mapping you do, the easier this will get.

Remember, plugging your ideas into existing forms is a generating technique: If they're not fitting, don't force them. That can be counterproductive.

An acronym looking for content

Once I was working on a story with some consultants who had come up with an acronym they wanted to push. First, they had the acronym, and then they tried to apply the content to the acronym. The approach struck me as the wrong way around. It's better to get your ideas down, get them into parallel language, and then come up with an acronym or acrostic. Not the other way around.

In my piece of work presented in Figure 2—Five qualities of a good idea—my acrostic is bad: NUCBZ. I say that the qualities of a good idea are <u>n</u>ovelty, <u>u</u>sefulness, <u>c</u>larity, <u>b</u>revity and a <u>z</u>inger/wow-effect. But NUCBZ is awful. My point here is this—what if I had tried to go the other way around? What if I had tried to make an acrostic based on the first letter of the word IDEA, NEW or SMART.

It might work, and I'm not saying don't try, but please don't force it.

Good articulation and writing are about finding the right thing to say, the right story to tell. It's about nailing it because the articulation rings so true. The reader had sensed what you're talking about before, but they hadn't articulated it. Because you did, that's very exciting.

In my learning-by-doing journey, I saw that my story-finding and story-framing process is valuable and usable to others. For the longest time though, even after I had begun to teach it to subject-matter experts, I wasn't exactly sure what it was. It was an implicit method I had been taught as a journalist, but I couldn't find any theory about it in all the old journalism textbooks I dug up.

The closest I got to a description of a story-finding method was guidance by William Blundell in his book

"The Art and Craft of Feature Writing." He said you need to consider these elements to frame the story:

* History
* Scope
* Reasons
* Impacts
* Countermoves
* Futures

This was good advice, and I began applying it, but it was still somehow hard to remember and wasn't sticking like I wanted it to.

That takes me to my next point: To come up with your own intellectual property, you may first need to borrow, apply and tweak.

Borrowing structures

For one of my pieces of intellectual property for this book, I looked at a company's graphical display of an idea and asked myself: How can my ideas be superimposed on a similar shape?

It was a scatter plot used by a strategy consulting company that caught my attention. I looked at the X and Y axes and saw how I could put two juxtaposed "end states" on each axis. So far so good.

Then I began to think about what comes in between the end states I had lined up. It took some tweaking, but I came up with this quality matrix about thought-leadership writing. (See Figure 7.)

Thought-leadership writing quality matrix

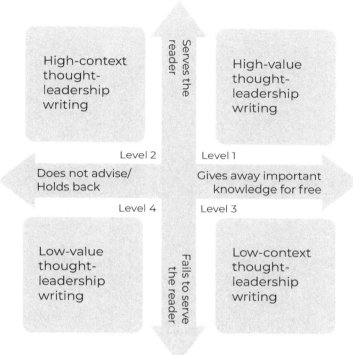

Figure 7—Thought-leadership writing quality matrix

Similarly, I created the next one by looking at the "to-from" states of my subject matter, which is writing. On one end of the spectrum, I put poor writing and on the other hand, compelling writing. Then I looked at what comes in between.

What is the spectrum you're working with? How can you apply your ideas to a similar form? (See Figure 8.)

Story quality matrix

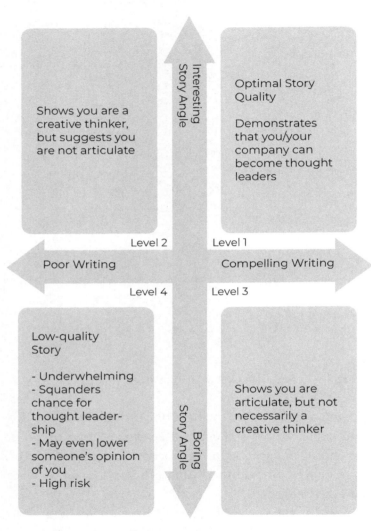

Interesting Story Angle

Shows you are a creative thinker, but suggests you are not articulate

Optimal Story Quality

Demonstrates that you/your company can become thought leaders

Level 2

Level 1

Poor Writing

Compelling Writing

Level 4

Level 3

Low-quality Story

- Underwhelming
- Squanders chance for thought leader-ship
- May even lower someone's opinion of you
- High risk

Boring Story Angle

Shows you are articulate, but not necessarily a creative thinker

Figure 8—Story quality matrix

Why create in the form of intellectual property?

What are the two matrices above good for? Why was I laying out my ideas in this way? For one, it was fun and different for me as a writer to create this way. Another reason is that this form of creating ideas:

- Keeps the ideas parallel, which makes me see faster what might be missing
- Helps me make the implicit explicit
- Helps others quickly grasp the context

There's another advantage: If I wanted to create a workshop or book chapter around these ideas, I could expand on them and would have new things to sell in my ideas-based business. That makes them very valuable.

New intellectual property comes from asking the right questions

To create new intellectual property, you not only need to brainstorm and then structure those thoughts, you also need to ask the right questions, or have them asked of you.

As a journalist, I keep lists of good questions to use for certain types of interviews. Similarly, I think there are a series of questions you can ask yourself (or be asked by someone else) that can lead you to generate your own nuggets of intellectual property.

Start with questions that help you articulate your area of expertise and the ideas you burn for.

Questions are:

- What do you know a lot about that matters to your audience?
- What is your unique viewpoint on your subject matter—e.g., what's right and what's wrong with what's going on in your niche?

Then move on to questions that involve your purpose, such as:

- Why are you pursuing this idea?
- How will your idea help promote the greater good on this planet?

Now, look at how you approach your work. Questions may include:

- What are some of the most important processes you perform in your niche?
- What types of end products or services are you involved in?
- What are the qualities of the product or service in the best case?
- What are the qualities of the product or service in the worst case?
- What are your personal best practices related to the processes you're involved in?
- What are others getting wrong about what you do?
- What are others overlooking?
- What is non-negotiable about the way you work?
- What about this is applicable outside your niche?

To become a thought leader in your niche, you will need skill in turning your own observations and hunches into meaningful, principled and actionable insights.

This isn't as difficult as it sounds. I think it's a lot easier to find meaning, principles and actionable insights when you're in conversation, particularly when someone is interviewing you with the goal of drawing these ideas out of the depths of your experience and understanding. For that reason, consider having someone else interview you using the questions above.

Cultivating the creative habit

As I mentioned at the start of this chapter, it's important for emerging thought leaders to be constantly generating new ideas. That means you need to cultivate the creative habit, as choreographer Twyla Tharp calls it in her excellent book, "The Creative Habit: Learn It and Use It for Life."

I like to cultivate my creativity with play, particularly word play. I participate in improvisation theater and experience immense joy with the language that players create on stage. It is freeing and exhilarating because of the new associations you're confronted with.

Improvisation theater is also a place where you can be raunchy, racy or even socially unacceptable if you trust your other players enough (and it's a closed-door practice session). It's the perfect environment to get the creative juices flowing.

I have rarely laughed as hard as I do in improvisation classes. And it became increasingly clear to me over the years that humor is critical to our human understanding.

Humor works because it reframes an idea and excavates a truth.

And truths are just what you need to be articulating when you're creating your intellectual property. Here's a joke that reframes:

> You've heard the one about the writer who was eager to get a job writing copy that would rally people to action? He wanted to put his energies into writing that made a difference in people's lives and got them up screaming and shouting.
> The writer finally found a job.
> At Microsoft.
> Writing error messages.

This joke which I heard somewhere is an example of what I mean when I say humor is critical for understanding. The surprise is the reframing of the typical understanding. And the humor works because of the truth. How many times were you just about ready to throw a punch at your machine? It's something you deeply understand.

Here are other things I do to get myself creating:

Feed. Consume those materials that are inspiring to you. "Quality in" means "quality out." I like to feed on the work of editor Shawn Coyne. I took his big idea nonfiction class, "The Story Grid Big Idea Seminar," which was over-the-top amazing.

Develop habits of solitude. Let's face it. The presence of other people, even the ones you love dearly, can break your flow and hamper your state of mind. When you're working alone, you decide when you start, when you stop, when you eat, when you sleep. That alone leads to a whole different experience than you can have when creating on other people's schedules.

Walk. Fresh air = a fresh perspective = fresh ideas.

Do repetitive and meditative tasks alone, such as cook, wash dishes or rake leaves.

Read outside your area. Way outside.

Capture your ideas. For me, the best capture methods allow me to capture, categorize and make notes all in one go. I pin a lot of websites and emails to my boards in Trello, a software that allows users to collect multimedia in lists that can be annotated. I use Pocket as well to collect articles and videos to watch. It creates a long list of content to consume that you can tag with your own keywords. I also print out quite a lot and place it into plastic sheet covers that are labeled with the idea/project I'm pursuing.

Commit to regular, personal deep work. For me, doing my own personal deep work on a regular basis means I'm able to harvest my heart, mind and soul for ideas. I get into rough patches and face my struggles in life and work, but I believe that if I continue with deep work with the help of a talented therapist, then things will eventually work themselves out (or I'll come up with a reframe that helps me see it that way.) By committing to staying healthy in this sense, I can commit to living a creative life.

Dredge it out with courage. Once I've done my searching and found pockets of ideas that I'd like to bring into form, I need to dredge them out like an archeologist would at a dig. This is when it's time to have courage and be honest about what you find. If the work you're doing is deep enough, then what you find won't always be pleasant.

Enable serendipity. I believe serendipity is an underrated part of the creative process. Serendipity deserves more status and acknowledgement for what it does. I also believe you can enable serendipity and cultivate a habit of inviting it into your process. When I articulated my Story-Framing System that you will soon learn about, serendipity was present. I had pulled up old slides from some of the first workshops I ever gave on feature writing, and just as I was trying to deconstruct my own process, one of those slides brought a breakthrough in my understanding, as I viewed it all in a whole new context.

Similarly, when I was in New York in 2019 getting the proposal for this book ready to show to agents, my concept wasn't 100% ripe. I happened to have bought an old Roger C. Schank book called "The Creative Attitude: Learning to Ask and Answer the Right Questions" on that same trip.

As I was working feverishly to tighten my concept, I happened to grab the book, read some passages and, by chance, I was able to move forward. Serendipity came my way, and I was open to receiving it. Serendipity had made fertile ground for new ideas.

Get an inbox pause function and stop ALL notifications. My last piece of advice for being more creative, accessing your best ideas and just feeling human in a hurried world is to turn off absolutely all notifications on all devices and use an inbox pause button to switch off email for a certain number of hours each day while you're in the act of creating. When you go back to see what's collected in the inbox, it's usually far less important than it would have seemed if each message had come in one by one, setting off a reaction from you and distracting you from your most important task—creating.

Key takeaways

- Everybody needs to gain skill in ideation and expressing ideas.
- That skill involves learning to sense and feel an idea, giving that feeling shape and then giving it form in language.
- By deconstructing your own processes—the "how" of what you do—you can create your own intellectual property.
- Sometimes it helps to apply your own ideas to borrowed structures to create new intellectual property.
- Having and articulating ideas is a joy and a key part of the human experience.

CHAPTER 4

Writing in the Thought-Leadership Style—A Quick Overview

To execute on thought-leadership writing, you need to take three steps:

> Step 1: Find it
> Step 2: Frame it
> Step 3: Flesh it out

This means find your thought-leadership niche, frame your thought-leadership stories and flesh out your ideas in writing. (See Figure 9.)

For Step 1, "Find it," you need to love your niche, live your niche, and own your topic.

People who stand out as thought leaders are those who are passionate about their niche and have used their curiosity and intellect to consider its problems and come up with ideas for addressing those problems.

If this description fits you, then most likely your attraction to a particular subject area is not a coincidence. That keen interest is probably born of your passion, purpose and expertise.

It's very difficult to identify an area out of the box and then "decide" you want to become a thought leader in that area retroactively.

Thought-leadership niches that aren't

For example, I might say artificial intelligence (AI) is an important field, and it will impact our lives significantly in the next decades. As a writer, it would make sense for me to specialize in how AI is impacting the way stories are told. Plus, I can't think of another person offhand who occupies this space in the realm of ideas. It's a wide-open niche looking for a thought-leader to occupy it. That would be yet another reason for me to go for it, right?

But if I use all this reasoning and go out and try to become a thought leader in this area, I will fail. That would be a rational decision, made in the head and not in the heart.

Indeed, I am interested in AI, and I'm very interested in the way stories are told. But at this point, I've barely investigated the overlap of these two subjects. First, I'd have to love it, live it and own it. With that passion and a mastery of the subject matter, then I have the chance to become a thought leader in that particular niche.

Framing and writing articles: An essential skill in business

I frequently work for professional services companies editing and writing their reports on a variety of topics, such as using wearable technology in the supply chain, or optimizing investment portfolios.

**Detailed version of the three steps to
thought-leadership writing**

STEP 01

FIND IT
To write like a thought leader, first you must define your thought-leadership niche, or the set of ideas you want to be known for.

STEP 02

FRAME IT
With your niche identified, now it's time to brainstorm story angles that will help you find new ways to express your ideas and make them more accesible to a wider audience.

STEP 03

FLESH IT OUT
Write an article born of your thought-leadership niche. Framed like a journalist would do it, in this story you share your knowledge and experience to help your audience solve important problems.

Figure 9—Detailed version of the three steps to thought-leadership writing

What I like about this crowd is that most of the people I encounter are super smart, ideas-driven and articulate. I learn a lot about a wide variety of subjects through interviews directly with the experts from the business. And when I get tough in my line of questioning, they are usually able to back up what they're saying. These people know their stuff inside and out.

However, experts aren't being given the skills they need to make their work understandable by general audiences.

They are frequently asked to write articles, but they aren't taught how to do so.

The communications departments cannot produce all the content themselves anymore, so it's quite common for experts to be asked by their organizations to write for publication.

When I edit their work, many of the stories that come across my desk present novel ideas in a way that shows deep experience and knowledge. That's great.

But more often than not, the stories aren't framed up in a way that makes them interesting.

Story angles that are old, worn and overused

If you offer a framed solution and deliver it to us in a way that is fast, doable and resonates with something we have all felt before, but been unable to articulate, we'll start looking to you for thought leadership.

That's where Step 2: "Frame it" comes in. It's about selecting the lens through which you will examine the subject matter, and I can't stress the importance of this enough.

For example, over and over again, I see stories that essentially have this angle: "Digital is here to stay, and your business needs a digital transformation."

In fact, this is a correct assessment. Digital is here to stay. And almost every company needs a digital transformation.

But that's not a story anymore because we all know it. That story angle results in a "here are the facts, ma'am" story.

The business world really does need smart advice on the topic of digital. There's quite a gap for thought leaders to fill. But they will have to get readers' attention with a better story angle.

This means they need to find a novel way into telling the same story or a fresh angle on why readers should listen to their message now. That could be a new proposition, a better way of working than what is usually done, or an opinion that is contrarian to what everyone thinks they know.

If you offer a framed solution and deliver it to us in a way that is fast, doable and resonates with something we have all felt before, but been unable to articulate, we'll start looking to you for thought leadership.

Ideas and the buzz they give you

A couple of years ago, I got an "aha" buzz from Michael Hyatt, a thought leader in the area of personal productivity, when I read one of his books in which he discussed the concept of "creating margin in your life."

Margin in your life means having buffer time to let life happen. It means having your "house" in order (he lists categories of "order," such as financial, relationships, health) and focusing on top priorities.

By doing so, you can avoid getting stressed out when the unexpected happens. It is an idea I have already explored in depth, but Hyatt's naming it "margin in your life" made the concept stick for me.

I believe that emerging thought leaders can distinguish themselves with interesting terms and phrases they create and by finding story angles that will resonate with their audience and enable them with deeper understanding.

Finding the right story angle

With the right story angles, you can keep the conversation fresh and lead the discussion to new territories.

How do you do that?

To find good angles about your core idea, you need to map out your ideas in a structured way to see their relationships and make new connections among the ideas.

That's part of Step 2, "Frame it," in the three-step process to thought-leadership writing.

Once you've identified your audience, then you begin to mind map their problems, both their internal problems and their external ones. This means mapping out the problems they know they have as well as the ones they may not really be aware of.

With fleshed out mind maps about problems faced by your core audience, then you look for ideas that are adjacent to your core ideas. The key word here is *adjacent*. With adjacent ideas, you can draw the reader in and give your idea set a new spin.

Back to the example of *"Digital is here to stay, and your company needs a digital transformation,"* that story you can no longer write.

If you find adjacent story ideas, you can have something new to say and wind up with a new reason to be issuing another call to action.

Your story might be:

- *Three reasons why digital transformation must happen from the ground up*
- or *Ways to handle employees who don't want to learn digital skills*
- or *Why it will take CEO leadership to move your company to the next level of digital*

All three of these headlines will take the reader back to the core message: Digital is here to stay, and your company needs a digital transformation, but they do so in a new and interesting way.

What story angles and photography have in common

The way we take photos is an easy way to explain story framing.

You compose the image in your view finder, deciding whether it will be center or off center, horizontal or vertical, portrait, a group shot or landscape. Snap. You take the picture and make a permanent impression. Similarly, when writing, the frame you choose will determine the composition of your story.

As discussed, *Digital is here to stay, and your company needs a digital transformation* isn't the right frame anymore. Before writing that story one more time, take fresh stock of your business landscape and the niche problem you are addressing in that landscape. Then imagine holding up a camera or an empty, wooden picture frame and deciding what goes into the composition and what stays out.

Framing stories well is the most difficult step of the writing process and an area where there's little imparted knowledge on how to do it properly.

Story framing is taught to budding journalists every day, but it seems mainly to be a learning-by-doing exercise.

The editor says, "Go out and get me a profile of the dog catcher in our town." And off goes the reporter. When they return to the newsroom, they've either got the story or they don't. The editor will let them know.

If the reporter didn't succeed in reading the editor's mind or framing the story up effectively on their own, back they go. It's almost as if teaching the art of story framing is something editors attempt to do through telepathy.

However, at some point, it clicks for journalists, and they frame stories left and right, as if in their sleep. They go through their day seeing

Story framing is taught to budding journalists every day, but it seems mainly to be a learning-by-doing exercise.

headlines and story ideas in their minds, and they already have thoughts about how to execute on their storylines. The more they write, the more proficient they become at structuring their stories.

Your WIP list, one of the most valuable things you own

You don't have to be a journalist to become proficient at framing. I'm confident you can become a story-finder in motion, utilizing quick and effective ways to capture story ideas so that you always have a long list to turn to when the time is right.

We journalists call this a WIP list, or a works-in-progress list. It's highly valuable. So valuable in fact that I remember that when one of my colleagues was leaving an international business newspaper for a different job, the editor wanted his WIP list. Those can be months in the making.

Flesh it out

Once you've got the right angle to a story—once you have the right photo composition or frame—you're ready to move on to Step 3, "Flesh it out," as in expand on your ideas in writing. This step is about sharing your unique viewpoint in a conversational tone.

To be seen as an agenda-setter or trend spotter, you must deliver your writing with simple, flowing language that mirrors the journalistic style. We'll discuss this more in Part 3 of the book.

17 types of thought-leadership articles

Thought-leadership articles tend to fall into two main categories: forward-looking or retrospective:

1. **Forward-looking** solutions articles are focused on how to solve the problem or be prepared for new problems and scenarios.

2. **Retrospective** solutions articles are focused on the historical analysis, or hindsight about why we have the problem in the first place.

In both, the goal is to inform about possible solutions. Most of these stories have a particular narrative type: explanatory.

Here are the 17 story types that I have identified (See Figure 10).

The 17 types of thought-leadership articles

Forward-looking

- Best-practices stories
- Explore-the-solution stories
- Applied-knowledge stories ("It's working there, try it here" stories)
- How-to-prevent-a-problem stories
- What-if stories
- Explore-the-trends stories
- Impact-of-the trend stories

Retrospective

- Understand-the-problem stories
- Reasons-why stories
- Share-my-process stories
- Myth-buster stories
- Why-I-believe stories
- Personal-impact and personal-experience stories
- What-really-happened stories
- What-surprised-me stories
- What-I-learned stories
- Simplify-the-complex stories

Figure 10—The 17 types of thought-leadership articles

Of course, the types of stories I list out here can also be used as story sub-structures in longer works. You might call those sub-structures "stories within stories." If they are anchored in time and place, then they might be anecdotes.

As sub-structures, these can be used in speeches, books or reports, for instance. You could even say that the chapter you just read was a "share-my-process" sub-structure in this overall structure, based on the Find it, Frame it, Flesh it out ideas we've been discussing.

Key takeaways

- Your niche subject must be an area that you love, live and own.
- It's essential to get a fresh angle to your subject matter to write about it in a compelling and interesting way.
- Thought leaders frame stories so they are useful, actionable and address the problems of their audience.
- Framing a story is like selecting a composition for a photo: To do it well, you need a fresh viewpoint.
- The 17 types of thought-leadership articles can be standalone articles or structures within a longer work.

CHAPTER 5

Find and Articulate
Your Thought-Leadership Niche

"MY WORKING HABITS ARE SIMPLE:
LONG PERIODS OF THINKING, SHORT PERIODS
OF WRITING"—ERNEST HEMINGWAY

To write like a thought leader, you first need to find your thought-leadership niche, and then you need to frame stories that emerge from that niche.

Finding your niche involves articulating your purpose and passion and then doing a wide capture of your unique ideas about your subject matter. To skip this step is to miss an important part of the process of writing the best-possible stories or books—the ones you were meant to write.

Besides, harvesting your mind and soul to find those ideas that you burn for, and finding your why, are among the most rewarding types of work. In my opinion, this leads to living and working in a more soulful way.

Emerging thought leaders get clear on their purpose

Even as I keep saying it's so important to do purpose-finding work before you begin writing, I did it late in my book writing process. I was already at my first writing retreat, about to dig in, when I finally put pen to paper to capture many of the personal stories and experiences that make me who I am today. It was immensely valuable, whether the ideas got incorporated into this book or not.

Finding your niche involves articulating your purpose and passion and then doing a wide capture of your unique ideas. To skip this step is to miss an important part of the process of writing the best-possible stories or books—the ones you were meant to write.

Therefore, I'll say it again. Please don't skip these first steps. "Purpose" work is your starting point.

How to find your thought-leadership niche

Finding your niche is a process in which you should depend on your gut instinct, while considering how you want to develop your business. This may be the business you already own, the future business you want to own, the company you work for, or the future company you want to work for.

Use the so-called law of attraction principle as you're defining your niche.

You're attracted to a certain set of ideas? Great. Follow them. See where they take you. As the writer and academic Joseph Campbell said, "Follow your bliss."

I created this model for defining your thought-leadership niche. That's the place from which you can write your best stories. (See Figure 11.) It is the intersection of three things:

- Your experience, expertise and/or your education
- Your passion and/or purpose
- Your unique viewpoint—for example, the big idea that you are developing within your subject area

How to articulate your thought-leadership niche

Figure 11—How to articulate your thought-leadership niche

Let's drill down briefly before expanding on these ideas later in the chapter. What do I mean by your experience, expertise and/or your education?

This is your subject-matter expertise. It is the subject you love, live and own. These are the ideas you burn for. Maybe the subject is something you taught yourself or something you majored in in college. But it doesn't have to be. The main point is that the subject is one in which you have deep experience because the idea set will not let go of you.

Ask yourself and do some freewriting about it: What do you know a lot about that matters to your audience? Your answer is the first component of your thought-leadership niche—your subject-matter expertise.

The second component of your thought-leadership niche is your passion and/or purpose. This is what's really driving you. These are your thoughts about what you want to change for the greater good on this planet.

If you reach your goals in spreading your ideas, in what way will the world be different and better? Your answer to this question links back to your passion and purpose.

Your unique viewpoint, or your big idea, is the third component of your thought-leadership niche. It is your unique perspective on your subject matter. Your unique viewpoint is based on your observations and experience.

Once you have identified these three components, where they overlap is your thought-leadership niche: I believe the best stories that you or your company can write are born from your thought-leadership niche. This is your story sweet spot.

Finding my own niche

When I began writing this book, I didn't know what my thought-leadership niche could be.

A few months before starting this project, I had laid yet another book idea to rest (the graveyard is full). I felt attracted to the idea of thought-leadership, and I knew it was a buzzword topic that could potentially be turned into a book.

At first, I wasn't sure how I would add to the existing conversation about thought leadership. It seemed like the literature already did an extremely good job of taking people from an idea to building a thought-leadership platform.

But as I did the exercises and applied the advice in the books to my own topics, which are ideation and writing, I began to realize that very little exists on *the actual writing of* thought-leadership materials. I began to see that what most books left out was where I could begin.

For years, I had been thinking about and articulating my ideas about what makes writing good, but not in a big way. I had given a few training courses and developed materials for those. But I didn't develop any of my own intellectual property until I worked through the books of Denise Brosseau and Matt Church et al.

I had been living and loving and owning my subject of good writing for a long time, but I hadn't structured my thoughts around my experience. I knew that I was enamored by good ideas and felt passion and purpose for this topic as well. So, with a burst of creative energy, and after months of reading on thought leadership and thinking about it, I sat down in roughly one weekend and wrote out the concept for this book.

When it flows, it pours

On a Sunday in my reading chair, I combined my experience as a professional writer for 25+ years with many of the things I had learned from working with consultants and running my own business, and I mined those ideas with tools from the books I was reading.

That session helped me structure many of my ideas. And let me tell you—it was so much fun. I get lots of joy from the ideation phase, and I had a ball with this one. When I was finished applying the authors' tips and techniques and doing their exercises, my ideas had a lot more heft.

Maybe you're thinking that I somehow had a head start, that you're not ready to sit down and write out a book concept. Believe me, I was there, too. And I stayed there for months and years at a time with multiple book ideas that never came to fruition and remain in my drawer.

What made this one different?

Timing. I think it was just the right time for me personally, the right idea, and the right time to fill a void that wasn't being covered on the topic. In my first round of conceptual work, when I created my Venn, I also applied that Venn to myself. I discovered that I want to be seen as an authority on thought leadership writing.

Once I knew the niche I was aiming for, many things got easier. I began to develop my manuscript and with it a base of ideas for my company, the Institute for Thought Leadership.

Ways to access your best ideas

Purpose work, understanding your "why," and accessing the buried ideas and stories that you carry around with you are important first steps in identifying your thought-leadership niche and opening the floodgates of the conceptual work that may sustain you for years to come.

I find five methods valuable for accessing and capturing your own ideas.

- Purpose work
- Freewriting
- Mind mapping
- Getting interviewed

- Chartifying, or juxtaposing ideas on a blank sheet of paper to see them differently than you usually do

The first two—purpose work and freewriting—fall into the category of deep access to your best ideas. The remaining three—mind mapping, getting interviewed and chartifying—are ways to uncover your subject-matter expertise. (See Figure 12.)

How to access your best ideas

Figure 12—How to access your best ideas

I recommend you use access methods in both categories, beginning with the two methods for accessing your deepest ideas: purpose work and freewriting.

After that, catalog your subject-matter expertise using mind maps, interviews and by chartifying.

Once you start writing down what you know, you may be surprised to see the volume, diversity and depth of your knowledge. If you have multiple areas of expertise, now is the time to capture them all to see any overlap or connections you hadn't observed and to organize the knowledge for safe keeping.

Purpose work and freewriting are ways to widen the search space to uncover your ideas—those that you had long ago that need to re-emerge, those you have suppressed, or those ideas that are in the process of taking form.

In contrast, mind mapping, list making and chartifying are methods of access that narrow the search space.

Access Method: Purpose work

Let's look at the first access method: purpose work.

Purpose work will help you access the ideas you have that aren't necessarily at the tip of your tongue. This method goes deep and requires soulful exploration.

For purpose work, I encourage you to work through whichever purpose exercises seem most appealing to you. I read Tim Kelley and Simon Sinek and did exercises they recommended. Looking back at my handwritten notes, here are some questions and prompts that got me writing down my thoughts. I have reconstructed them here:

- Write down or tell an interview partner 10 short stories from your life.
- Capture how you felt when those things were happening.
- Identify themes in those stories, or have your partner help you do so.
- Based on the themes that emerge, write down a statement that captures your why and what impact that why will have.

Whichever prompts you choose to work with, write down the answers, don't just tell someone. It's likely you will capture important nuggets of your own knowledge and ideas in that writing or list-making.

Stuart's purpose work

After completing my own purpose work, I did a purpose-finding exercise with my client Stuart.

Being a coach and leadership trainer himself, Stuart was relatively clear on his purpose. He was developing his ideas about wisdom technologies.

We used the "What If? Future" (WIF) exercise from Denise Brosseau's book, "Ready to Be a Thought Leader? How to Increase your Influence, Impact and Success." She describes a WIF as "a single, simple, striking description or image of the future you want to see."

"All thought leaders need a WIF. They may not yet be sure how to get there, but an inspiring WIF can attract followers and galvanize them to take action," she wrote. Using Brosseau's template, I asked Stuart to describe the future he imagined, the difference he wants to make, what he wants to eradicate, and what he wants to change.

Here's our interaction:

Q. What future are you committed to make happen?
A. Businesses need to have a set of tools that generate non-linear and deep insights into themselves, their customers and societies to enable them to make choices to benefit all.

Q. What change do you want to see happen?
A. That businesses have the courage to look at themselves more deeply and the wisdom to try new things.

Q. What must happen?
A. We need an awakening and an awareness in businesses and society to develop a sense of responsibility and ensure that they work with a connection to soul.

Q. What must you work to prevent from happening?
A. I want to stop people from reacting with cynicism and doubt. This type of change is hard and involves venturing into the unknown. Some companies have not been willing to take the journey, so they are not part of a networked and meshed view of the world.

Stuart's work in this purpose exercise may have led to a new idea he can develop in an article, or it may have helped him get clarity, which is always good for your writing.

A professor of mine often said, "Clear writing comes from clear thinking." I agree.

I also believe that good writing comes from life, and being a student of yourself and your life will help you find and articulate the ideas you want and need to share. You may not know what those ideas are right now. Purpose work can help you find them, and what you find may be surprising.

Access Method: Freewriting

General freewriting is another great way to find out what you think about a subject and let ideas collide to see which new ideas germinate post-collision. It's also a great way to find stories for your business and begin developing pieces of intellectual property, such as processes or best practices.

Here's an example writing prompt for you to use:

Tell about a time and place when you suddenly knew everything was different. What was it that you left behind? What were you headed toward?

Another idea is to criticize the work of key authors in your niche during a freewriting session. By taking a book to task, you can understand key works in your field better and see where your ideas differentiate.

Or try writing the author a letter you'll never send, saying why you think he or she is right or wrong. This will help you evolve your ideas and spur your own thinking.

For instance, asset managers looking for new ideas for their own business or investment portfolios can take the latest book on investment strategies and portfolio construction and carry out a written debate with the author of the book. The author will have already presented their main arguments in writing, so that makes your job easier.

Here are some more freewriting prompts for you to try. If it helps you begin rolling, start with brainstorming a list in response to the prompt. Then expand on an idea in that list with freewriting.

- Write about your gift and the message you have to spread.
- Write about the story you are telling yourself about something related to your work or life.
- Tell about a time when you were unstoppable. Where were you? What were you doing? What made you unstoppable?

Harvesting your purpose work and freewriting

When it comes time to harvest your purpose work and freewriting, make sure you can distinguish the original from what comes after that. As you look for the gems, use a different colored pen to make your notes and complete your sentences. This allows you to know what came out during the first draft, which are your purest, rawest, and most truthful ideas vs. what came out during the reading and editing.

You see, the judge in all of us loves to self-edit. At least with a two-toned text, you'll be able to know when you were writing without the judge in your head getting his say too much.

I realize you may be thinking, "Hey, this is a book about business writing. Why am I working on such deeply personal topics in purpose work and freewriting?"

Leaders need to be clear on what they think and why they feel certain ways.

Purpose work and freewriting offer you ways to get closer to your own personal truths and the messages you have to share with the world.

Access method: Map it out

To access your subject-matter expertise, I recommend mind mapping, getting interviewed and chartifying.

Mind mapping is akin to making lists with sub-lists, like an outline. Each level of sub-list is another arm out on the mind map.

In contrast to outlining, mind mapping may make it easier to see mistakes in hierarchy that you have built into your ideas, or to visualize conceptual gaps.

If you are burdened by too many ideas that are bouncing around in your head like popcorn, a mind map is a good way to apply structure. It can have a calming effect. Mind maps also have a positive effect on writing because mind maps separate thinking from writing, which leads to better structure in your writing.

When a mind map starts getting too complex or too full, break out a higher-level mind map that puts your ideas into buckets or categories that are one level of abstraction higher. If that is still too complex, do it again. Once the higher-level maps have structure, then continue drilling down on lower-level maps.

Access Method: Get interviewed or facilitated

Another way to access your ideas about your subject-matter is to get interviewed, preferably by someone who is a skilled interviewer yet doesn't know much about your work.

That person will have to ask basic questions to get oriented, and answering those questions is good practice for any expert.

By seeing which questions the interviewer needs to have answered, you can better understand where other listeners are coming from.

I don't recommend writing out specific, detailed questions in advance—that could lead to a stale interview. Just sit back and let the interviewer do their work in leading a natural conversation. When you are finished, have the interview transcribed. Then see what you had to say in written words instead of spoken words. You might be surprised by what you find in the transcript.

Here are some ideas of things to touch on in an orientation type of interview:

- Who are you as an expert?
- How did you arrive at the topic you love so much?
- What makes you love it so much?
- How do you see things differently than others in your niche?
- What is the big picture of your work or the big change you're advocating?
- How do you propose to make it happen?

In a second step and second interview, you can drill down on one or two ideas that emerged from the first interview and explore that area for subject-matter expertise and potential nuggets of intellectual property.

Looking back at the transcript, did anything you say surprise you? Did anything become clearer to you because you had to explain it to someone else?

In my coaching sessions, I do a lot of interviewing to understand the ideas the person I'm coaching is trying to articulate. When I first started coaching, I couldn't decide whether to wear my journalistic interviewer hat, my coach hat, or some form of both. Each form of questioning is different.

The reality is that the approach must be tailored to the intended result of the interview.

If I'm interviewing an expert to ghostwrite an article, for instance, on best practices for the transition from LIBOR rates, then I must wear the journalistic interviewer hat.

I must lead strongly, I have to dig, I have to interject with questions. I have to make sure it all makes sense, and I am getting the full story with enough examples and detail to give the story its sea legs. I'm the one who is going to decide what's important and relevant. At least in the first draft.

In contrast, when I'm coaching someone in finding their thought-leadership niche, or we are hashing out their book outline, story outline, or chunks of intellectual property, then I need a more delicate approach. I'm there as a sparring partner and listener, and I should be more of a facilitator than a guide with a right to cull ideas.

When you're in the process of identifying the subject-matter you want to run with, it's best to get facilitated first to ensure that someone doesn't edit out your most precious ideas. If the interviewer has a strong hand, you may end up generating something that doesn't sit 100% with you.

Later, once your subject matter is clearly identified and it's time to build out your ideas, get interviewed by someone who is really digging to help you refine and structure your ideas.

Access Method: Chartify

I once pitched my editors at BBC Capital a story on creating charts to organize your thoughts and your life. Ever since a client of mine sent the briefing as a chart years ago, asking me to write up a certain story based on the information in the chart, I had seen how useful charts are that organize and juxtapose ideas.

Charts will:

- Help you visualize the gaps in your raw information and thinking
- Force you to articulate that missing information
- Help you keep ideas parallel

I am still deeply impressed by Atul Gawande's book on checklists, "The Checklist Manifesto: How to Get Things Right." At the time of my pitch to BBC Capital, I had been thinking about how I could create a similar ode to one of my favorite tools, the chart.

Unfortunately, I didn't get very far with my pitch, even though I was one of their steady writers. It's quite common that it takes three or four full-fledged pitches to land a single assignment at the BBC. But it didn't stop me from continuing to use charts or thinking about them.

In the books I read on thought leadership, the authors suggest creating a chart to capture everything that is wrong with your field, a list of "sins." This is a way to drill down on your knowledge and the areas in which you or your company can offer solutions.

I liked that idea, so I went at it on that Sunday afternoon in my reading chair. Here are a few of the "sins" I came up with for thought-leadership writing. (See Figure 13.) Later, I organized the ideas by category—they are either "sins" of angle, or "sins" of execution.

Try it with your own material:

- Begin a chart and brainstorm everything that is wrong with your niche.
- Then go back and make the language in your list parallel.
- In another step, see if the "sins" you generated fit into categories.
- Finally, as the expert in this area, you've thought about how to improve things. Note down some of your fixes for the "sins" in the column to the right.

Here's what I did with the topic of poor writing in companies.

"Sins" and fixes in a niche

Example: "Sins" and fixes in business writing—short version

	"SIN" TYPE	A FIX
"Sins" of story angle	Author comes across as having nothing new to say	Find what's new about this topic. Go from the small to the large, or large to small to see it in a new perspective.
	Story is about a subject that isn't really your business	Find a different story to tell.
	Basic idea of the story doesn't serve the reader	Bring in the reader's needs and pain points. What are the internal and external challenges the reader faces? Put them on a mind map.
"Sins" of story execution	Author is holding back their knowledge	Realize that it's hard to give away too much in short form, so start giving away your best ideas.
	Story has a slow start	Use the journalistic process of teasing out what's new in the lead to avoid an academic style with a preamble.
	Story talks down to the reader	Stand back and reconsider your audience and tone. Rewrite.
	Story moralizes	No one wants to hear from someone who is ranting and moralizing. Just stop it!
You can find the full chart of business writing "sins" in Part 3. Continue with your ideas here.		
Place a "category" of "sin" in your niche below	Place a "sin" in your niche below	Write your fix below

Figure 13—Chart of "sins" and fixes in a niche (Example: "Sins" and fixes in business writing—short version)

I had fun creating my "sins" chart above. Had I tried to explore those ideas without a chart, I don't think they would have come out so clean and with parallel language, which is a must.

Chart brainstorming is an excellent way to structure thoughts about emotional matters as well, because a chart can force you to boil down a complicated matter into a few lines of essence. I once actually did it for a relationship: In one column, "He said ..." In the second column, "He may have meant ..." In the third column, "How I understood what he said ..."

Try a three-column idea-development chart to unearth story ideas or food for thought. (See Figure 14.)

Below I have started a chart around unspoken truths in business writing, the truth as I see it, and the ideal end state, as it relates to thought-leadership writing.

Unspoken truths in thought-leadership writing

UNSPOKEN TRUTH IN BUSINESS WRITING (State the false belief here)	ACTUAL TRUTH AS I SEE IT (State that truth here)	THE PREFERRED/ IDEAL STATE (Write the ideal situation here)
Companies believe that they will gain traction in the market by producing lots of content about what they do.	Companies need to steer away from low-value content and instead find and tell the right stories to engage clients in important conversations and raise sales.	Subject-matter experts deeply involved in the business have great ideas and stories to tell. They need story smarts to help them articulate their ideas in ways that engage clients and prospects.
Now copy this chart and insert your observations for your area.		
Unspoken truth in your niche, organization or industry (State the false belief here)	Actual truth as you see it (State your truth here)	The preferred/ideal state in your niche or organization (Write the ideal situation here)

Figure 14—Three-column idea-development chart (Example: Unspoken truths/beliefs about thought-leadership writing)

Chartify unspoken truths

Here's another one.

Let's say you're a financial advisor and you want to write a blogpost about money psychology and how it impacts personal money management. You want to share with your clients some tips on how to bring their investment account balances to the next level by overcoming their limiting beliefs.

You have already done the purpose exercises and understand your deeper motivations for tackling the subject. Now you want to mine your experience and ideas for material and solutions to help people build their nest eggs.

In hundreds of hours of advising clients, you've heard so many reasons why an investor cannot do this or that. You grab a blank piece of paper and begin to write down limiting beliefs in the left-hand column of a chart and a corresponding positive affirmation in the middle column. (See Figure 15.)

For each juxtaposed statement, you can use your client experience to develop several story ideas that address the problem. Place those headlines in the third column.

Here is an example using the topic of money beliefs, something that an expert in financial planning or wealth management could use for their business.

Juxtaposed ideas chart with corresponding story ideas
Example: Money beliefs

LIMITING BELIEF ABOUT MONEY (State the limiting belief here)	AFFIRMATION ABOUT MONEY (State the positive belief here, as if it had already come true)	HOW AN EXPERT COULD APPROACH THE TOPIC IN A STORY (Write a possible headline here)
I don't really have enough to invest more.	I have plenty of money to save and invest.	*Thinking traps: Why it's easy to believe you don't have enough to invest*
I can't negotiate raises for myself.	I am a strong negotiator who regularly gets raises for myself.	*Three ways you may be sabotaging your next raise*
Making a large salary would indicate I'm greedy.	I earn substantially because I'm paid what I'm worth.	*Under-earning? This may be the reason why*

Example: Data analytics

LIMITING BELIEF ABOUT DATA ANALYTICS (State the limiting belief here)	AFFIRMATION ABOUT DATA ANALYTICS (State the positive belief here, as if it had already come true)	HOW AN EXPERT COULD APPROACH THE TOPIC IN A STORY (Write a possible headline here)
Data analytics is too difficult for a small company to do.	With the right tools and processes, small companies can use analytics better and quickly find niche advantages against larger competitors.	*Three ways small companies can put data analytics to work today*

Now copy this chart and insert your ideas:		
Limiting belief related to your subject matter (State the limiting belief here)	Positive belief related to your subject matter (State the positive belief here, as if it had already come true)	Your approach to addressing the matter (Write a possible headline here)

Figure 15—Juxtaposed ideas chart with corresponding story ideas (Examples: Money beliefs and data analytics for small companies)

Similarly, a chart that juxtaposes is excellent for generating best practices that you can share with readers.

In the left column, capture the problem faced in a project or the client's general problem. In the middle, capture what you or your company did about it. On the right, formulate the lesson learned that might be applied elsewhere. The below example could be from a consulting company. (See Figure 16.)

Fill this out for many of your clients' problems and look for conversations you can have or stories you can write.

Problem/ Action/ Lesson-learned chart
Example: Client segmentation project done
by a consulting company

CLIENT PROBLEM	ACTIONS TAKEN	LESSON LEARNED OR ILLUSTRATED
Our client's segmentation of its own customers was too rigid, leading to inflexibility in the supply chain.	We (the consulting company) developed and rolled out a new classification system for our client's customers that captured more detail.	Companies need more granularity in segmenting their own clients to work more flexibly with them.
Continue with your ideas here:		
CLIENT PROBLEM	ACTIONS TAKEN	LESSON LEARNED OR ILLUSTRATED

Figure 16—Problem/ Action/ Lesson-learned chart (Example: Client segmentation project done by a consulting company)

Here is another chart to use in the research phase of your writing, particularly research for long-form writing. (See Figure 17.) It allows you to catalogue and compare ideas and state succinctly how you agree or disagree with the ideas of others.

In the left column, write down the names of works you referenced. In the middle column, place some of the key ideas of those other works.

In the third column, write down your reaction and how your work could be different than the input literature. Capture what you agree with in the other works, how you see things differently and questions to pursue.

Chart of ideas in similar works and input literature
Example: Other books on thought leadership

BOOK NAME AND AUTHOR	MAIN IDEAS	MY REACTION
"Ready to Be a Thought Leader?" By Denise Brosseau	To become a thought leader, you need to understand your why, codify your ideas and build a following of people who are working together with you for the greater good.	Excellent work with great exercises that helped me begin seeing my own work differently Doesn't say much about writing, just that you need to write often and well
"The Thought Leaders Practice" by Matt Church et al.	Individuals can scale up their thought-leadership practices by getting multiple service lines (clusters) going and enabling that work to cross-pollinate itself. It's possible to earn well, while doing work you love with people you like.	A great guide to increasing your earnings by selling your thoughts Packed with useful ideas and tips Doesn't say much about writing, just that you need to write often and well
"Accidental Genius" by Mark Levy	You can find and develop your own thinking by developing a practice of freewriting.	An ode to the process of freewriting packed full of prompts and tips Hard to believe Levy uses freewriting in companies, but it's a great idea. I'd love to see it happening more often.
Now copy this chart and insert your reactions to others' work:		
Book name and author of a similar work or input literature for your project	Main ideas of that work	Your reaction to the work

Figure 17—Chart of ideas in similar works and input literature (Example: Other books on thought leadership)

If you're working on a book manuscript, or developing workshops, a product or a service, try this chart to generate ideas about the value transformation and shifts you are enabling and selling. (See Figure 18.)

Chart of value shifts and transformations you're enabling or selling
Example: Rhea's workshops and book

THE "BEFORE" STATE OF MY AUDIENCE	THE SOUGHT-AFTER STATE OF MY AUDIENCE (USUALLY ASPIRATIONAL)	ENABLING TRANSFORMATION TO THE SOUGHT-AFTER STATE
Example: Rhea's workshops		
Workshop participants are subject-matter experts who want to learn how to articulate their ideas better, write better and be heard in a crowded marketplace.	Participants gain confidence that they have great ideas to serve their audience that need to be uncovered and articulated in ways that make them readable and useful.	I help people see themselves and their own ideas in a new light.
Example: Rhea's book		
Readers believe that idea generation and writing are some of the hardest things they are faced with. When they begin my book, they feel daunted by the writing task they have set out in front of themselves.	Readers feel the task at hand has become more doable and are inspired to get out there and try it themselves.	I provide practical tools that can be applied immediately. I share my own journey.
Now copy this chart and capture the transformation you're enabling:		
THE "BEFORE" STATE OF MY AUDIENCE	THE SOUGHT-AFTER STATE OF MY AUDIENCE (USUALLY ASPIRATIONAL)	ENABLING TRANSFORMATION TO THE SOUGHT-AFTER STATE

Figure 18—Chart of value shifts and transformations you're

enabling or selling (Example: Rhea's workshops and book)

Chartify the transformation

Ideally, your readers, participants, clients or users will undergo an experience of "transformation" by interacting with your work. This is where you can capture that proposed transformation succinctly.

A good book coach, for instance, may ask you as a writer to articulate the "before" state of your reader as they begin each chapter and the "after" state you want that same reader to be in when they are finished with the chapter.

By forcing yourself to articulate the shift you want to enable, you can more clearly see if you have achieved your goal in writing the chapter.

In the chart above, write the "before" state of the audience in the left column. In the middle, write the sought-after state, and in the last column, write how your writing, product or service enables transformation to the sought-after state. The examples below are from my business.

If you are already advanced in your conceptual work and know some of your main messages and points, capture in a chart the stories and examples you will use to make your points come alive. (See Figure 19.)

Doing this in a structured way helps you see what you have and where it may fit in long-form pieces. You can brainstorm directly into the chart or capture what you've already written into the chart.

Anecdote and example chart for organizing long-form work
Example: Rhea's book

MY ANECDOTE OR EXAMPLE	MAIN POINT OF THE ANECDOTE OR EXAMPLE	WHERE COULD THE ANECDOTE OR EXAMPLE FIT IN MY WORK?
Story about my narrative nonfiction work that was never published (page 6)	We are all scared of the process of writing and publishing, and many of us have big failures behind us.	Introduction
Example of an overused story that consultants still try to write: *Digital is here to stay, and your company needs a digital transformation* (page 72)	Even if what you're saying is accurate, it may not be the best angle into the story. You need to find new and fresh ways into the story to deliver the same message that still needs to be driven home.	Chapter 4 on writing in the thought-leadership style
Anecdote about meeting a doctor with story ideas who I thought I couldn't help (coming up on page 115)	Because experts are focused on their niches, most of them need help framing their stories to make them actionable and usable for a general audience.	Chapter 6 on story framing
Now copy this chart and insert your own collection of anecdotes or examples, as well as the point they illustrate:		
Your anecdote or example	Main point of the anecdote or example	Where could it fit in your work?

Figure 19—Anecdote and example chart for organizing long-form work (Example: Rhea's book)

Now that you have done purpose work and harvested so many of your ideas, it's time to pull that all together and articulate your thought-leadership statement.

Articulate your thought-leadership niche

Your thought leadership statement captures your aspiration of thought leadership and grounds it in your purpose and expertise.

You may want to go back and review the three parts of the Venn shown in Figure 11 (on page 81) about your thought-leadership niche, which is different than a thought-leadership statement.

Your thought-leadership statement captures your aspiration of thought leadership and grounds it in your purpose and expertise.

As discussed, your thought-leadership niche is your story sweet spot. It is the place to find story ideas because it is the intersection of your passion and purpose, your expertise and your unique viewpoint.

Below I walk you through creating your three-part thought-leadership statement. (See Figure 20.)

If you are an independent business owner, use the format on the left side of the figure, which is also printed here.

Fill in the sentences started below:

1. I want to be seen as an authority in:
    (Insert the niche topic that you burn for.)

2. because I ...
    (Insert your higher goal, such as the greater good you seek related to your niche topic.)

3. which will ...
    (Insert your very practical business, personal or career goal.)

If you are employed or a job-changer, use this format, which adds the phrase "In my organization" to the beginning of the statement:

1. In my organization, I want to be seen as an authority in:
   (insert the niche topic that you burn for)

2. because I ...
   (insert your higher goal, such as the greater good you seek related to your niche topic)

3. which will ...
   (insert your very practical business, personal or career goal)

The whole template is below.

Articulate your thought-leadership statement

You are an:
Independent Business Owner/Feelancer

(1) I want to be seen as an authority in:
(insert niche topic that you burn for)

_____

_____

(2) because I... *(insert higher goal/greater good you seek related to niche topic)*

_____

_____

(3) which will... *(insert practical business/personal/ career goal)*

_____

_____

You are
Employed/Job Changer

In my organization/ future organization,
(1) I want to be seen as an authority in:
(insert niche topic that you burn for)

_____

_____

(2) because I... *(insert higher goal/greater good you seek related to niche topic)*

_____

_____

(3) which will... *(insert practical business/personal/ career goal)*

_____

_____

Figure 20—Template to articulate your thought-leadership statement

Articulating part 1

Here are some edited examples of thought-leadership statements from participants in my workshops.

> "I want to be seen as an authority in digital communications for social impact campaigns …"

> "I want to be seen as an authority in finding opportunities in a crisis …"

> "I want to be seen as an authority in using ancient Oriental wisdom to resolve modern business challenges …"

> "I want to be seen as an authority in the prevention and resolution of personnel conflicts in the workplace …"

Now write down your part 1 statement.

Articulating part 2

Next is part 2 of the statement. Write why you want to be seen as an authority in a particular subject niche. That's the "because I" part of the statement.

This second part is not so easy to state because it links back to your purpose, which might still be nebulous.

Try to phrase it as the positive change you seek at a societal level.

Here's what I'm using right now for part 1 and 2 of my thought-leadership statement:

"I want to be seen as an authority in story framing and writing in the thought-leadership style because I believe the world already has so many solutions we need for big problems, but those solutions are stuck in experts' heads ..."

Articulating part 3

In part 3 of your statement, strive for an ordinary statement about how your work will boost your career, your visibility in an organization or your own business.

Here are two completed statements (parts 1-3) from workshop participants that I've synthesized and tightened:

This is from a person working with non-profits:

"I want to be seen as an authority in digital communications for social impact campaigns to help social justice leaders shine in communications because I want to help them create more equitable, thriving communities. This will build my business and enable me to live the life I want to live."

This one is from a consultant in an independent practice:

"I want to be seen as an authority in using ancient Oriental wisdom to resolve modern business challenges because I want to help humanity renew its ways to achieve health, happiness, harmony and higher levels of consciousness. This will build my business as an advisor."

A well of stories, born from your thought-leadership niche

The above statements give you an idea of an articulated thought-leadership niche. I see such statements as life-long works in progress: You can ponder and tweak them frequently.

With your statement articulated, you've got a clearer understanding of all areas that make up your thought-leadership niche.

That's a good thing because your niche is exactly the place we'll go scouting for stories in the next part of this book.

The stories we'll find there will be born of your personal thought-leadership niche. They won't be story ideas generated by a machine or a communications department working in isolation from you, the expert.

These stories won't just be regular, hollow stories that are optimized to make search engines happy. They'll be the opposite of industrialized content.

Your stories will resonate with your passion and purpose. And they will draw from your deep expertise to serve your audience. As a result, your stories will position you as the go-to expert in your niche.

Key takeaways

- Your thought-leadership niche is the intersection of your passion/purpose, your expertise and your unique viewpoint.

- It is also your story sweet spot—the place to find stories that will serve your audience and resonate with them.

- Once you have explored and structured your key ideas through different access methods, such as freewriting and chartifying, you're ready to articulate your thought-leadership statement.

- Your thought-leadership statement is an aspirational statement that captures your area of authority, your reason why and your career or business goal.

PART 2

FIND YOUR THOUGHT-LEADERSHIP STORIES

CHAPTER 6

Story Framing: The Art of Making Your Ideas Relevant

"THE ROOT PROBLEM IN MOST AIMLESS WRITING IS THE
FAILURE TO RECOGNIZE THE DIFFERENCE BETWEEN
A TOPIC AND AN IDEA" —JACK HART

In my work, I've encountered many experts with important things to say who have struggled to make their ideas relevant, interesting and usable for their audiences. If you feel you have genuinely unique ideas but are not being heard and recognized for them, you're not alone.

How do you make yourself memorable as an expert?

It's with your ability to generate new thinking on well-worn subjects and bring across those ideas crisply and clearly. No one is asking you to create something completely new or think about it in a completely new way. To rise to thought leadership, what you need is a fresh take on a problem that many people have been contemplating a long, long time.

You can dramatically improve your chances of being seen and recognized as the go-to expert on your subject by getting the right story frame for your ideas.

To put it another way: If there is any leapfrog technique available to quickly and drastically improve your writing, it's getting the right story angle for your articles, papers and books.

As I often say, if you are a consultant working with digital technologies, you can no longer write an article called
"Digital is here to stay, and your
company needs a digital transformation." Similarly, if you're
a scientist and you're sharing
a set of facts with your readers
without showing them why your
subject is important, why now,
and why you care about it, your
story will be hard for a general audience to digest.

If there is any leapfrog technique available to quickly and drastically improve your writing, it's getting the right story angle for your articles, papers and books.

Getting the story out of the expert's head

Over the years, I have interviewed thousands of experts as
sources for my journalism pieces and my corporate work.

When I go into the framing interview for a story, I typically need to do a warm-up with the expert.

These are the type of questions I begin asking the
expert:

- Who is your reader?
- What is your intent with the story?
- What is your business interest in writing the
  story? (This can be different from the intent,
  which may simply be to educate/explain)
- What is the reader's main problem you're
  addressing?
- What is unique about your solution/approach?
- Has your solution been tested?
- Do you have experience implementing your
  solution?

If the person doesn't know what they want to talk about specifically, then I mention places that are fertile ground to look for stories.

Often, I like to say, "If you were asked to give a keynote about your niche at the biggest industry conference of the year, what would it be about? What would be the title of your speech?"

Here are some places individuals and companies can begin looking for ideas to share. Story ideas may be a part of:

- Your opinion
- Your knowledge
- Your process
- Your criticism (of methodologies/ conclusions)
- Your advice
- Your reactions
- Myths that need debunking
- Best practices
- Ethics in your niche

These are all good places to consider something you may want to share that relates to a problem you care about deeply. Knowing these locations to harvest is a good starting point.

The trouble with "Here are the facts, ma'am" stories

A few years ago, I started offering business story consulting as a standalone service. To my surprise, a doctor called me up asking for a story-finding session on her subject: cancer prevention. I had met her privately and she had begun to read my posts on LinkedIn. From what I could tell, she had already looked in some of these places to find stories. She had "mined" her knowledge to find out what she wanted to write about.

But when she called me, I was a bit perplexed. Why was a doctor reaching out to me when she knows I write a lot of tech and finance and have a background penning articles on workplace psychology, leadership, motivation and other such subjects? Frankly, I tried to dissuade her from booking the consultation with me.

As we were getting into the subject, I asked her to send me some sample articles she had written. She forwarded me a piece about breast cancer screenings that basically had this storyline:

- Breast cancer is the main killer among cancers in women.
- It's easy to catch early if you get the screening done.
- All women over a certain age should get their screenings done regularly.

As I read that, I suddenly realized that I could help the doctor find a more interesting angle for her piece. She had lots of things going for her. She had the knowledge and credentials, and she felt very strongly about contributing to society with this message. But what she showed me was a "here are the facts, ma'am" story.

Even if I were sitting in her waiting room with nothing else to do, I wouldn't have read that story.

Tantalize with the new

Why not? Because I already know that story, at least in the way she presented it. Reading the headline did not release any hormones in my brain that caused anticipation and made me want to read the article.

But I do need help in this area, just like most women. The doctor could certainly help me, but she only had one chance to get my ear, and with that story angle, I simply wouldn't give it.

We proceeded with our discussion, and I began to ask the doctor about her personal experience. What do her patients say? How does she manage her own self-exams and screenings? How does she speak to her teenage daughters about it?

During the discussion, we came up with new and different ways to give the same core message which is this: Ladies, get your screenings done.

Some of the headlines we came up with were:

- *How to turn your breast screening appointment into a lunch date with a friend*
- *Can't bring yourself to do your self-exam for breast cancer? Here are my hacks.*
- *Three mental blocks to doing your breast exam or screening*

A fresh angle shows fresh thinking

So how did we go from a breast-cancer prevention message and a typical storyline (*Breast cancer is the main killer among cancers in women*) to these three headlines, which indicate a different approach to the material?

This is where the editor's telepathy comes in.

Journalists simply know how to make this leap after asking a few questions "around" the subject matter, seeing what has already been written and considering the audience and purpose of the story.

Because they have written so many stories and understand the ingredients needed to write a good story, they instinctively go for a new, interesting, or fresh angle. If they don't? The editor will pass or send them back to the drawing board.

In corporate publishing and when writing in the first-person, thought-leadership style for your own business, the task is the same: to find a story angle "around" the original subject and approach the material from a whole new direction to explore potentially new meanings or understandings.

Other uses of the term "framing"

Like most journalists, I am constantly storifying. However, when I look back at my education and training, I realize that I was only taught how to do it with a "learning-by-doing" approach. I don't recall ever having much theory about the process.

In journalism textbooks, you'll find info on "nut grafs" or finding the right "impact" to explore a given news item, but there is very little on story framing, in the sense of finding the right angle to tell the story.

Story framing in business writing means finding a way to jump from your identified subject and intended message to an interesting way to bring both across in a story.

In other domains, the term framing is used differently.

In journalism, "the way the story is framed" can refer to the conscious or unconscious bias the writer has in selecting the news angle. For example, someone might question with which frame a story about the Persian Gulf war was written. If the writer consciously or unconsciously saw the Persian Gulf war as one that was fought to liberate the Kuwaiti people, the story might reflect that frame. If the writer consciously or unconsciously saw the war as one to secure oil production for outsiders, the story might reflect that frame.

In politics, framing the conversation can mean "spinning" the conversation or choosing the best rhetorical frame for persuading others of your point of view, with or without regard to the facts, as the linguist George Lakoff explores in his books and talks.

> *Story framing in business writing means finding a way to jump from your identified subject and intended message to an interesting way to bring both across in a story.*

In the study of power dynamics, frame is used in the sense of "viewpoint control." Authors like Oren Klaff talk about ways to control the frame after inevitable frame collisions.

In behavioral economics, the "framing effect" that psychologist Daniel Kahneman describes is the cognitive bias that leads people to make choices based on whether those choices are presented with positive or negative connotations.

In psychology, framing is about the mental models that enable people to see patterns, predict how things will unfold and understand new situations. As machines become smarter, humans still have an advantage because only we can frame ideas, say the authors Kenneth Cukier, Viktor Mayer-Schönberger and Francis de Véricourt.

According to Wikipedia, "In the social sciences, framing comprises a set of concepts and theoretical perspectives on how individuals, groups, and societies organize, perceive, and communicate about reality." In this sense, story framing in thought-leadership writing does just that. Once you've framed your story, you've chosen a way to communicate about reality as you see it.

In general, the important thing to keep in mind about the difference between journalistic articles and thought-leadership articles framed with journalistic techniques is that journalistic articles should have no commercial intent.

They are feature or news articles designed to inform, educate and serve the reader, but they should not be pushing any particular product or service to do that. If they are, then it's not journalism. Yes, some serious newspapers run these types of stories, but they're printed in special sections that are designated as advertising.

Thought-leadership articles, on the other hand, do have a clear commercial intent.

Accounting for my process

When I set out to understand how I was generating journalistic storylines for articles published by companies, while others were struggling to do the same, I began to deconstruct the story framing interviews I was conducting with my clients on a regular basis. I wanted to find out the method behind what I was doing.

Here's what happened in a story-framing session for an article about two accounting definitions that are being used interchangeably, even though the two terms aren't interchangeable.

The expert I was interviewing had observed the problems that the two definitions were creating and wanted to forewarn his clients about them by writing a story.

This is what I did in the framing interview.

First, I sought to understand:

- The problem
- The interesting and newer aspects of the problem
- Examples of the problem
- The causes of the problem
- The consequences of the problem
- What could happen if the problem isn't solved
- How widespread the problem is
- Examples of proposed solutions to the problem

As I gathered this information, I was thinking ahead about how I might structure such a story and what type of story it might be.

When the story structure became apparent to me during the interview, I began to interview along that storyline. But first I had to understand the above to get the story going at all.

Here are some of the headline ideas we eventually came up with:

- *Why "default" and "credit-impaired" are not the same*
- *The risks of using "default" and "credit impaired interchangeably*
- *How jumbled jargon—even when everyone else is using it—leads to noncompliance*

From topic and message to a fresh story angle

Here's another example of taking a subject and a message you want to write about and turning them into a journalistic story angle that presents the idea in a new or simplified way.

Let's say you're a consultant working on a story about high-speed internet, 5G, and how it will give industrial companies the boost they need to make the internet of things (IoT) a reality in their production halls.

Finally, with these networks up and running, machines will be able to gather and transmit data in near real-time. IoT will work as it was envisioned.

Someone writing this article might work for a company that sells advice on whether to build your own network for your factory or hire a telecommunications provider to do it for you. In other words, they advise on the telecommunications industry and have an opinion on the build vs. buy dilemma.

Considering this, your readers will already know that 5G is right around the corner. Telling them that it is coming isn't a story. That is like a "here are the facts, ma'am" story, in the same way the original version of the cancer-prevention story was.

Instead, consider some of the elements William Blundell talks about in "The Art and Craft of Feature Writing":

- **Widen the scope** of your story by asking: What will be possible with IoT once 5G arrives?
- Explore the **impact** by questioning: How do companies assess their readiness for production with 5G and IoT?

- Examine the **future** by asking: What are the implications on production planning from 5G and IoT?

Based on these questions, here are some headlines for the 5G story that make the leap from "here are the facts, ma'am" to an interesting story angle:

- *Three new things you'll learn about your own production once 5G arrives*
- *When 5G meets IoT: Will you be ready?*
- *How production planning will change when 5G gives IoT the boost it has been waiting for*

These are story ideas I just made up based on my own knowledge of IoT. Imagine what's possible when a journalist has a subject-matter expert to guide them in the story-framing process? Together, they can find story angles on every street corner.

Similarly, an expert empowered with journalistic story-finding abilities can create a long list of engaging stories to write. That long list can be the antidote to the problem of needing to communicate the same message repeatedly to benefit your business.

Consider Simon Sinek, the purpose-finding expert. He talks about purpose repeatedly, and his followers eat it up. Sinek didn't invent the concept of purpose, but he does a fantastic job of making purpose relevant and accessible for thousands of people. He brought in his own ideas and experience, and, most importantly, he finds good frames for those ideas that enable him to keep his audience engaged over the long term.

Above I have shown you the results of a few story-framing sessions with experts. Now I want to share with you at a more detailed level how I generated those headlines. There's more to it than just asking yourself the questions that Blundell suggests.

To capture the method I inherently use, I began to listen to myself in recorded story framing and story-finding sessions so I could figure out what the heck I was actually doing. It took some time to capture the method, but I have done so now in my five-step process for framing thought-leadership stories.

What is story framing in business writing?

Story framing is the process of reducing an idea to a headline to make the story easily understandable for others and yourself.

The goal of an initial story framing session is to generate a working headline that gives you clarity on what the story is about.

In a story-framing session, you define the frame or composition that you will use to discuss the select ideas that have made the cut this time around.

Notice the word "cut."

Yes, story framing is about the refined discretion of knowing what to bring in and what to leave out. If an idea doesn't fit into the frame you have selected, it's gotta go.

Not everything can fit into each piece. That's difficult for many experts to accept, since they've often worked very hard at generating the ideas and concepts in the first place. Rest assured, though, leaving things out is a critical part of story framing, and doing so takes courage and practice.

Putting an idea into headline form makes the idea tangible and actionable for the writer who needs to write it. A headline serves as an "enabling constraint." Like haiku or Twitterverse, the limitations of the form also provide its opportunities.

Once you get the story down to a headline, it's usually much clearer how you should execute that story. And that clarity is often what subject-matter experts lack because they have been working with their ideas so intensely for so long.

A chartered financial analyst (CFA) in one of my workshops brought up this point. She had framed up a "three reasons why" story for herself during our story-finding exercise, but she felt the headline was too cheesy for her sophisticated audience of institutional investors.

A headline serves as an "enabling constraint." Like haiku or Twitter-verse, the limitations of the form also provide its opportunities.

I empathized and suggested she use the headline as a working title to keep clarity on the structure of what she would be writing. Then, in a final step, she could kick out the first headline and replace it with a new one. Most likely, during the writing process, she would come across a new headline idea anyway.

The Five-Step Story-Framing System

The goal of framing stories born of your thought-leadership niche is to find fresh ways to talk about a subject that you want and need to talk about repeatedly.

As a quick review of Part 1 of this book, stories born out of your thought-leadership niche reflect your passion and purpose, your expertise and your unique viewpoint on your subject, as shown in the Venn diagram in Figure 11 (on page 81).

Where these three areas overlap is your story sweet spot, because anything you write from that spot will naturally have depth and meaning for you and therefore resonate with the right audience.

That means that the stories we are creating here are the opposite of the hollow, formulaic ones that fly by night on the internet. This story-finding exercise leads to articles that are authentic and purpose-driven: Your headlines will be the opposite of the algorithmically generated ones that some content farms are already using.

With that in mind, let's turn to the five steps. (See Figure 21.)

> Step 1: Map your business, subject or research **landscape**
>
> Step 2: **Map your niche** within your subject area
>
> Step 3: **Map the problems** in your niche
>
> Step 4: Map **only one problem faced by your audience** in your niche
>
> Step 5: Considering the **story type**, create **headlines** touting your solutions

Story framing and zooming the lens

Framing a story is like finding the right composition for a photo you want to take.

Like photos, each story is a cut out, a moment in time, a snapshot within a much wider context. And that's by design.

When you do a step-by-step story-framing process, imagine that you're looking through a camera lens and adjusting it like a photographer would do. The goal is to focus in on a very specific story you want to write, after having considered the larger context.

Sometimes a photographer doesn't know exactly what she is going to photograph at the beginning, so she starts

The Five-Step Story-Framing System

Figure 21—The Five-Step Story-Framing System

looking through her lens for something that catches her eye. Then she adjusts the lens, zooming in little by little.

By zooming in, she finally focuses her camera on something very specific that shows a creative way of looking at the landscape.

That something specific is the composition of your story—what you will write about.

Your headline is what you would call that story—it's the frame you put around your composition.

Ideally, since you're writing stories to promote your business, the composition you choose for your story (e.g. what you've zoomed in on) and the frame you set it in (e.g. the headline for your story) will relate back to a solution that you or your company offers.

Below is a summary of the five-step process for framing stories, as seen in Figure 21.

Into the top of the funnel, in the first two steps, you put context and understanding about your business, your audience and their problems. Along the way in steps 3 and 4, you examine the audience's problems and drill down on one of those problems in great detail.

Finally, toward the bottom of the funnel, in Step 5, you use headline templates to create a frame for an article you want to write that showcases your solution or set of solutions for a particular problem.

Finding adjacent stories for content marketing

What is essentially happening with this five-step system?

My Story-Framing System helps you find stories that are *adjacent* to your core idea so that you have a fresh take on your subject matter and another reason to repeat the implicit message about your business.

That's what I did with the doctor. A story like *Six mental blocks to actually doing your breast screening* is *adjacent* to her core message, which is "Ladies, get your exams done." She has both a fresh take on the subject and a reason to repeat the implicit message about her business.

As she publishes more of these type of stories, people will begin to associate the doctor with that area of expertise.

Similarly, *When 5G meets IoT: Will you be ready?* is a story idea that is *adjacent* to the consulting company's message, which is "It's difficult to make the buy vs. build decision for 5G networks. Better get some extra help on board."

Story-finding in my subject area

Let's run through the process again, this time with my subject matter as an example.

We've already talked about the thought-leadership niche I've articulated for myself based on my experience, my passion and purpose, and my unique ideas. Here it is again: "I want to be seen as an authority in thought leadership writing, story-finding and ideation because I want to help experts articulate their best ideas to solve some of the world's biggest problems. Doing so will help me build my business, put my kid through college and live the life I want to live."

Since I'm clear on my thought-leadership niche and goals, I'm ready for Step 1 of the framing process.

Step 1: Map your business, subject or research landscape

Here's my business landscape. This is important for you to know to understand how the headlines I'm generating will support my business goals.

For this step, use a mind map to create a visualization of your business for yourself, or use a list. That mind map or list should catalogue the type of work you do.

Here's my list.

At my company, we offer: workshops on ideation, messaging, thought-leadership and story-finding, among other services.

Since I've mapped my business landscape, I'm now ready to move on to Step 2.

Step 2: Map your niche within your subject area

Here the goal is to select and zoom into an **<u>area</u>** from your Step 1 map, where you or your company can say "yes" to each of these questions:

- ☑ I am **passionate** about this topic and know a lot about it.

- ☑ My **audience** has a **burning need** to know more about certain aspects of this topic.

- ☑ **I need more visibility** as an expert in this area to reach the next level of my business.

This is your subject-matter niche.

Again, use a mind map or list and start writing down your niche for your own business.

Make it as specific as possible.

In my case, my subject matter niche is writing in the thought-leadership style. Not just writing, and not just thought leadership, but writing in the thought-leadership style.

That is the subject I'm interested in right now, no matter how I deliver it. I can say yes to the three questions above, and this is the area where I believe I can make an important contribution.

Knowing my subject-matter niche, I'm now ready for Step 3.

Step 3: Map the problems in your niche

Here it's important to work with a mind map and not a list because now we're zooming into your business landscape to focus on your audience's problems to which you, as the thought leader, have the answers.

Now place the words "Problems in" in front of your subject-matter area and put that into the heart of your mind map.

For instance, if you are an expert in agile project management, write "Problems in agile project management" inside the center of the mind map.

Here's my problem statement for my Step 3 mind map. (See Figure 21a.)

Place your general problem set in the center of your Step 3 mind map

Figure 21a—Place your general problem set in the center of your Step 3 mind map

My niche is thought-leadership writing. So, I plug "Problems in thought-leadership writing" into my mind map, and then I begin to catalogue the problems I have observed.

Important: It is the problems you want to map here, since the articles you write are going to offer solutions.

Here is my expanded Step 3 mind map detailing problems in thought-leadership writing. (See Figure 21b.)

**Build out the arms of your general
problem set in your Step 3 mind map**

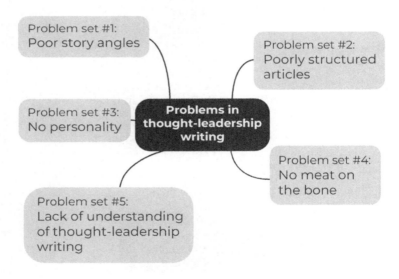

Figure 21b—Build out the arms of your general problem set in your Step 3 mind map (Example: Multiple problems in thought-leadership writing)

Here's an expanded version of what's in my figure above presented as a list for easier reading. I made several more levels of the mind map that are not visible in the figure above.

Problems in thought-leadership writing:

- Problem set #1: Poor story angles in articles written by subject-matter experts
    - Nothing new to say
    - Buried main point
    - No opinion
    - Too much discussion of the problem—not enough focus on solution
    - Too much discussion of the solution—not enough focus on the problem

- Problem set #2: Poorly structured articles
    - The initial build-up to the main point takes too long
    - Wandering ideas
    - Irrelevant examples/anecdotes

- Problem set #3: No personality in the writing
    - It lacks humor
    - The story sounds like it was written by a machine

- Problem set #4: No meat on the bone
    - Story includes filler ideas and words
    - It doesn't present anything new
    - Story is vague
    - It doesn't add to the discussion

- Problem set #5: Lack of understanding—what is thought-leadership writing
    - Thought-leadership writing isn't a sales pitch
    - Thought-leadership writing shouldn't be blah
    - Thought-leadership writing isn't recycled ideas of others

Now we're ready for Step 4.

Step 4: Map only one problem faced by your audience in your niche

Zoom further and drill down into one important problem. It's best if you choose a problem that really interests you and one for which you have lots of solutions. I chose poor story angles as my problem in thought-leadership writing. It is located on the upper left hand of my Step 3 mind map. (See Figure 21c.)

Zoom into one problem in your Step 3 mind map of general problems in your niche

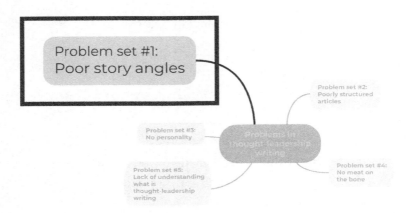

Figure 21c—Zoom into one problem in your Step 3 mind map of general problems in your niche (Example: Poor story angles in thought-leadership writing)

Now I want to really look at this problem of poor story angles in depth by putting this problem at the center of my next mind map.

I want to break down the problem of "poor story angles in thought-leadership writing" into components of the problem.

This Step 4 mind map is the key mind map in the entire Story-Framing System.

State the problem as a sentence in the middle of your mind map and begin to look at the problem from as many directions as possible as you break it down.

- What is the problem on the surface?
- What is it under the surface?
- What are the roots of the problem?
- What is the impact of the problem?
- What will happen if the problem continues unabated?

Here's my problem stated as a sentence:

Subject-matter experts use poor story angles or the wrong ones in their writing and fail to hold the attention of their readers.

That now goes into the center of my fresh Step 4 mind map, and off I go capturing problems I've observed when subject-matter experts write for general audiences but without proper story framing.

Again, make sure you choose a problem you know a lot about and can help solve.

Also very important: Choose only one problem and only one audience, otherwise, the exercise will become confusing. If you have more than one problem you want to address, and you have more than one audience, that's OK.

Breakout each problem faced by one audience separately in multiple mind maps. Then take it to town. You can have as many mind maps as you want, just make sure you've only got one problem and one audience in each centerpiece.

Here is mine. (See Figure 21d.)

Move one problem faced by your audience to the center of this new mind map for Step 4

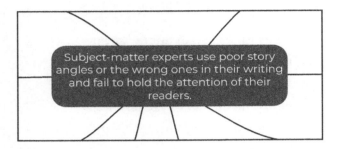

Figure 21d—Move one problem faced by your audience to the center of this new mind map for Step 4 (Example: Subject-matter experts use poor story angles in their writing and fail to hold the attention of their readers)

Then fill out the mind map.
See how I have done that here.

Slice of a filled out Step 4 mind map

Figure 21e— Slice of a filled out Step 4 mind map (Example: Subject-matter experts use poor story angles in their writing and fail to hold the attention of their readers)

Below is what's in this mind map as a list.

At the center: Subject-matter experts use poor story angles or the wrong ones in their writing and fail to hold the attention of their readers:

Here's what you'll find on the arms of the mind map:

- **The story has an overused angle**
  - Story is something we've heard a thousand times before
  - Expert may be following a "broken" template for story structure provided by their firm
- **The story has an old angle**
  - Story doesn't show creative thinking
  - Story doesn't move the conversation forward
- **The story has a boring angle**
  - Angle is not necessarily old, but still somewhat standard. Not intriguing
  - Reading the headline does not lead to a release of dopamine (e.g., does not awaken anticipation)
- **The actual story is buried in the story**
  - New and best ideas introduced in the final "key takeaways" of the article
- **The story angle is not something that really resonates with the writer**
  - Even if it's a good story angle, if the writer is not interested in it, the story will be flat
- **The story lacks opinion**
  - Writer is too afraid to share an opinion
  - Writer doesn't have an opinion to share
  - Opinion too commonly held
  - States the obvious or the widely accepted
  - Opinion too big for a person of his or her stature

- **The story says nothing new**
  - Expert is too used to recycling material
  - Expert has been left alone without training and support in discovering their best ideas and new ideas
- **The story has no journalistic angle—It's a "Here are the facts, ma'am" story.**
  - Story presented in an academic style or reads like a list of ideas

Here's a template for you to use for your Step 4 mind map with your own ideas. (See Figure 22.)

This is a breakdown of one problem faced by your audience. Choose only one audience. Important: Choose a problem you know a lot about and can potentially help solve.

Template for the most important mind map in the process, your Step 4 mind map. This is a breakdown of one problem faced by your audience

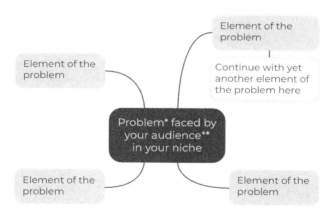

*Choose a problem you know a lot about
**Choose only one audience

Figure 22—Template for the most important mind map in the process, your Step 4 mind map

Now we're ready for the fifth and final step, Step 5, which does not involve a mind map.

Step 5: Considering the story type, create headlines touting your solutions

This is where you will see how to "apply" your solutions as headlines, using headline templates.

For each articulated problem you worked on in Step 4, consider **types** of thought leadership stories you could write. Types may be:

- A share-your-process story
- A best-practices piece
- Or a myth-buster story

In most cases, multiple types of stories can fit a problem that has been mapped well.

In Chapter 4, I listed out 17 types of thought-leadership stories. (See Figure 10 on page 76.)

Let's chartify a few of those types, together with the problems I articulated just now, to see what could fit together. (See Figure 23.) This is a step for you to do intuitively as part of Step 5.

Chart for considering which story type fits
with a problem you're addressing

PROBLEMS WITH THOUGHT-LEADERSHIP WRITING (FROM MY STEP 3 MIND MAP)	TYPE OF STORY/STORIES THAT COULD FIT
Problem: Writing has no meat on the bone	• How-to-prevent-a-problem story • Share-my-process story
Problem: Writing has no personality	• Share-my-process story
Problem: Writing has a wandering structure	• Share-my-process story • Impact-of-the-trend story • Best practices story
Problem: Writing/story has a poor angle	• Best practices story

Figure 23—Chart for considering which story type fits with a problem you're addressing (Example: Thought-leadership style stories)

The above exercise is the first phase of Step 5—consider possible story types. Again, do this implicitly.

With these possible story types in mind, I can now begin applying my headlines, e.g., touting my solutions to the problem of poor story angles in articles written by subject-matter experts.

Typical headline types

How do you tout the solutions you have as a headline?

First, have a look at some headline templates.

Here are six categories and examples, based on headlines from feature stories I wrote over the years. Note: My story editors wrote most of the headlines, as is typical for these publications. And these are headlines for feature stories, which are reported stories that differ from thought-leadership stories. But the headline types still illustrate the point here. (See Figure 24.)

141

Headline types – Examples From Rhea's Stories

#1 Numbers
10 ways to... 5 secrets for... 7 reasons why...

Four ways to save more of your paycheck
Forbes

#2 How to + Action (do something) + Unique benefit

How to induce sleep without drugs
BBC Capital

#3 Highlight mistakes

Speechless: Three big mistakes of public speaking
BBC Capital

#4 Clever language

Business Schools Set Course For Charted Waters
WSJ

#5 Questions

Is your colleague pure evil?
BBC Capital

#5 Bold statements

Take your power back from a control freak
BBC Capital

Figure 24—Types of headline structures that can be used in thought-leadership writing

Now consider how you can combine the problems you have articulated in your Step 4 mind map with a solution expressed using a headline template—for example, as a question, bold statement, using numbers or highlighting a mistake?

Just start playing with it and have some fun. See what pops out.

Coming up with a catchy headline isn't as daunting as it may appear. In my short-form workshops, we do a turbo version of this, skipping to a Step 4 mind map. We do the problem mind maps, I show the headline templates, and off people go.

Remember to put yourself in the eyes of the reader and offer solutions in the form of headlines.

Did the headline you wrote grab your attention or speak to you? If not, try again. Is it too long-winded? If you wouldn't pick up the story with that headline in your field of expertise, than trust me, neither will another reader.

Below is a chart designed to make the results of the framing session we just walked through clearer. It uses problems from both my Step 3 and Step 4 mind maps.

Your goal is to generate headlines like those in the third column for your own subject matter. (See Figure 25.)

Chart of story ideas generated with The Story-Framing System

PROBLEMS IN THOUGHT-LEADERSHIP WRITING	TYPE OF STORY/ STORIES THAT COULD FIT	POSSIBLE HEADLINE/ STORY ANGLE/ SOLUTION YOU'RE TOUTING	HEADLINE TEMPLATE USED (See page 142)
Problem: Writing has no meat on the bone	How-to-prevent-a-problem story	*Three ways to deepen any story you write about your business*	#1 Numbers template
Problem: Writing has no personality	Best-practices story	*The Write Way: Bringing your personality to the page* or *You're not a dud. Don't make your writing one either*	#4 Clever language template
Problem: Writing has a wandering structure	Explore-a-solution story	*How nut grafs can help keep your story on track*	#2 How to + Action (do something) + Unique benefit
Problem: Writing/ story has a poor angle	Share-my-process story	*With this story-framing process, you'll never write another boring story again*	#6 Bold statements

Figure 25—Chart of story ideas generated with The Story-Framing System (Example: Thought-leadership writing)

Here again are the story ideas I generated in the third column:

- *Three ways to deepen any story you write about your business*
- *The Write Way: Bringing your personality to the page*
- *You're not a dud. Don't make your writing one either*
- *How nut grafs can help keep your story on track*
- *With this story-framing process, you'll never write another boring story again*

With these headlines, I now have new and interesting ways to say the same point I need to drive home: To become a thought leader, you need to write like a thought leader. And one quick way to improve your writing is to get a better story angle.

You can also use these headlines across your communications, for instance as:

- Email subject lines
- Sub-heads (shortened)
- As social media tidbits
- In visuals
- As names for podcasts or videos
- In your marketing copy
- As the basis for a product name or service offering

Generating a constant stream of story ideas

As you get your ideas out to the world to promote your business, research or solution, you'll need a constant stream of stories to keep your audience engaged. Here are some tips to keep the headlines rolling once you've begun to find them.

- Repeat The Story-Framing System, selecting a different part of your business in Step 1.
- Repeat it for Steps 2, 3 and 4 as well, using different components of your niche and generating different problems in that niche.
- Break down the one problem you select for Step 4 in new or different ways. If your problem relates to people, consider their internal struggles and their external struggles and do a separate mind map for each of these.

If your list of story ideas to write becomes too large, consider categorizing them, perhaps for a very narrow segmentation of your audience or around a particular step in your process.

For example, on my editorial calendar for the weeks and months ahead, I have headlines categorized under the three steps to thought-leadership writing: Find It, Frame It and Flesh it Out. If I realize my audience wants to know more about Find It, I can pull up a story idea to write that will support that particular step.

If you are independent or changing jobs, I could imagine that your audience might even enjoy voting on which story you should write next. You could put three headlines to choose from into a poll and see what your audience wants next.

One caution here when you're creating headlines. Don't overpromise and underdeliver in your headlines. Make sure you have the knowledge on tap to deliver on your selected framing. Otherwise, your headline will seem like clickbait.

Blundell's framing advice

Another way you can generate headlines is to apply Blundell's framing advice, which I have chartified below to make it applicable to headlines.

His technique is different than the one I have shown you, but it can also work well if you are creating story ideas based on your thought-leadership niche. (See Figure 26.)

Chart for applying William Blundell's framing advice
Example: Thought-leadership writing

GENERAL PROBLEM ADDRESSED: WRONG OR POOR STORY ANGLES IN ARTICLES WRITTEN BY SUBJECT-MATTER EXPERTS		
BLUNDELL'S FRAMING ADVICE:	**POSSIBLE HEADLINE:**	**COMMENTS:**
Narrow the viewpoint (of the subject)	*My single biggest reason for framing the story before I write*	Here I narrowed to only one reason.
Widen the viewpoint	*Why good story angles are a key ingredient for building a thought-leadership platform*	Here I widened to bring in the broader idea of thought-leadership platforms.
Look for outliers	*Three surprising things about thought-leadership writing*	I call out the outliers.
Look for outliers (more)	*People say you must be a good public speaker to be a thought leader. I say you must be a good writer.*	I present an outlier.
Examine trends	*Thought-leadership writing is getting better every day.*	
Examine trends (more)	*How to know when your company has gotten off track with its thought-leadership writing*	
Consider motivations	*Why quality writing for thought leaders suddenly has the spotlight*	
Consider the impact	*No imparted wisdom, no business: If your content has no depth, customers will shun it—and you.*	
Same goal, new path to get there	*Want well-written content about your business? Hire a journalist at your company.*	
Same goal, new path to get there (more)	*Why you should retain an ideas coach*	
Historical view	*How thought-leadership writing evolved over the years*	
Look for analogies	*If content is king, then writing is its head servant.*	

Figure 26—Chart for applying William Blundell's framing advice (Example: Thought-leadership writing)

Here are my story ideas in the chart as a list:

- *My single biggest reason for framing the story before I write*
- *Why good story angles are a key ingredient for building a thought-leadership platform*
- *Three surprising things about thought-leadership writing*
- *People say you must be a good public speaker to be a thought leader. I say you must be a good writer*
- *Thought-leadership writing is getting better every day*
- *How to know when your company has gotten off track with its thought-leadership writing*
- *Why quality writing for thought leaders suddenly has the spotlight*
- *No imparted wisdom, no business: If your content has no depth, customers will shun it—and you*
- *Want well-written content? Then hire a journalist at your company*
- *Why you should retain an ideas coach*
- *How thought-leadership writing evolved over the years*
- *If content is king, then writing is its head servant*

That's a long list of story ideas I need to get busy writing.

Nailing the hook in longer works

Until now, we have been talking about finding angles or hooks for first-person, short-form articles.

For longer pieces, such as books, you also need fresh angles, and you'll need multiple fresh angles. Your umbrella concept will need one, and under that, the ideas you drill down on in each section will also need fresh angles.

That means for longer works, you may want to use The Story-Framing System multiple times. If you are developing a book meant to position yourself as a thought leader, you need to funnel your conceptual energy into what editors call the hook. This is the sentence or two that summarizes how you are addressing the reader's pain point.

In prescriptive nonfiction, which is often what emerging thought leaders write, it is your hook, your "how," that will make your book stand out as different. And this hook belongs on your cover and in your sub-title.

The hook should convey the big idea behind the story but also be a statement that is tailored. Ideally, it will have a wow effect.

In scanning The New York Times best seller list, I found some sample hooks printed on book covers and in book descriptions:

- "Talking to Strangers" by Malcolm Gladwell
  - Hook: "Famous examples of miscommunication serve as the backdrop to explain potential conflicts and misunderstandings"
- "Sapiens: A Brief History of Humankind" by Yuval Noah Harari
  - Hook: "How Homo sapiens became Earth's dominant species"

- "The Body Keeps the Score" by Bessel van der Kolk
  - Hook: "How trauma affects the body and mind, and innovative treatments for recovery"

These short titles and statements are the result of months and probably years of work clarifying and distilling the main idea in a work. They are deceptively simple and extremely useful.

Story framing and return on investment (ROI)

I recommend reading and studying titles and hooks to help you gain more skill in framing stories—whether you're writing articles, papers or books. As your skill increases, you'll also wind up saving yourself time and energy during the conceptualization and writing process.

Here's why I say that. Recently, a consulting company sent me stories for editing that hadn't been framed by the business consultants before the writing, nor by an editor or someone from the communications department.

I've changed the industry here to protect the client, but some of the stories that came across my desk for editing had headlines like this:

- *Don't run in circles*
- *Analytics at work*
- *The next generation of process excellence*

The above are topics, not storylines. If a writer sets out to write about a topic instead of a story idea, they may be able to narrow the angle to get vast amounts of information under control, but they will probably still be lost in the thick of it.

That's what Jack Hart was talking about in the opening quote for this chapter. He says you've got to distinguish between a topic and an idea. A topic is something you might want to look into some day. Your article should not be a "look into" some vast subject. Instead, if you have a story idea, it will have a filtering effect in the form of a hypothesis. That's what you need to move forward.

In this case, a partner had come up with the story angles related to the business and then assigned the juniors to write those stories. Perhaps the partner thought it would be too expensive or time consuming to have story-framing discussions with an editor or communications person before the subject-matter experts started their writing.

Little did the partner realize that having a framing discussion with a writer or communications person before the writing begins saves both time and money. That's because the professional editor who will look over the articles at the end of the process will have to change a whole lot less if the stories are well-framed from the get-go. Stories will not be sent back to the expert for a rewrite, after being bloodied by the editor's red pen.

Without a framing discussion, my experience shows that the editing needed on the stories is heavy. They are chock full of good detail, packed with solutions to the client's problems, and show that the writer has deep knowledge gained from experience. That's all very admirable.

But the stories often have these problems:

- The story's lead is buried.
- The weighting is off: The story is 80 or 90 percent about a well-known problem, and the solution gets short shrift.

- The story is too wide: It stays on the surface about a whole gamut of solutions or problems, and it doesn't do any sort of deep dive. Usually, this means it is a lot less useful.
- The story sounds like it was written by a committee.

Often, the story touts a solution to a pressing problem but hardly explains how the solution works. The main point ends up being "we have a solution you should be interested in," but the detail is so lacking that the reader begins to wonder if the firm or person actually has that solution, or it has only been conceptualized.

These are problems that can take some time to fix. Why not head them off with a story-framing discussion in advance? Your communications department or your sparring partner in this conversation should be able to help you tease out what's new or different in the story you want to tell.

Whatever that nugget is, it belongs high up in the story or in the headline. That's what will make your piece a conversation starter with your audience. Book descriptions put the big idea of the book on the cover.

What's your new idea in the article?

Once you've found it, lead with it.

Key takeaways

- Story framing is the process of finding the lens through which you want to tell the story.
- A story frame is a reflection of reality as you see it.
- One of the best ways to improve your writing quickly is to find better story angles.
- Headlines for your stories help you visualize the structure of the story.
- When a story is framed in a journalistic way, it will not come across as a "Here are the facts, ma'am" story.
- By constantly finding fresh angles to explore your subject matter, you can serve readers while still repeating the main message you need to be sending for your business.

PART 3

FLESH IT OUT: EXPAND ON YOUR IDEAS IN WRITING

CHAPTER 7

Ready to Write

"A LIMITED TALE WELL TOLD HAS MORE IMPACT AND
PERSUASIVENESS THAN A SWEEPING STORY THAT CAN'T
BE ADEQUATELY ILLUSTRATED" —WILLIAM BLUNDELL

Now that you've framed your story, it's time to put pen to paper. Since you framed your story in a journalistic way, you've already got a strong start.

Remember, everyone has a story to tell but how you tell it makes all the difference between successfully drawing readers in or having their eyes glaze over.

This chapter and the final chapter walk you through the 17 types of thought-leadership stories, highlight writing "sins" to avoid, and share tips and tricks on the writing process and mindset.

Thought-leadership writing and storytelling

Like thought leadership, the term storytelling has become a buzz word in business with many different interpretations.

Storytelling can be used to describe:

- How to articulate a concept in the most engaging way that resonates with your audience
- Workshops or the process of learning to tell better stories

- Story finding, even though story finding and storytelling are different things
- A tool used for organizational change or leadership development

The truth of the matter is that writing in the thought-leadership style and storytelling in business overlap. They do so on the level of the narrative arc. Story framing is how you structure and set up the story, while the narrative arc is how you execute that structure using writing techniques that create tension as the story progresses.

Stories of transformation

Often, the push for better storytelling in business is an effort to highlight the transformation that you as a leader, your company, your customer, your product or your service, has undergone.

Stories of transformation are one of the most valuable and useful types of stories to tell because when done right, they show a vulnerability in what happened as a result, whether positive or negative.

> Story framing is how you structure and set up the story, while the narrative arc is how you execute that structure using writing techniques that create tension as the story progresses.

This inevitably leads to arcs of tension throughout your story because the reader wants to know how things panned out.

As the writer Tom French has said, "The three most beautiful words in the English language are: 'What happened next?'"

When the result of confronting a challenge was positive, the storyteller may be providing a service to the reader by sharing best practices. If the results were negative, which is nothing to be ashamed of, the story gives readers insight on how to avoid making similar mistakes. Both techniques can be used in first-person thought-leadership writing.

Your daily dose of the hero's journey

A commonly used narrative arc is the hero's journey. In business writing, it requires focusing on the turning points related to your subject. If you're writing about a project, your scientific research, or the development of a product, that's a process that surely had ups and downs. These ups and downs are where you look for turning points you can share about in your narrative, either within its larger structure, or at the level of the anecdote.

When writing in the first person for your business, you can borrow from the techniques used by authors of reported works, memoir and even fiction.

Here are some questions you can ask yourself, as well as prompts for freewriting to generate story ideas or parts of articles. They are inspired by some of the steps in the hero's journey:

- In what areas of my work am I battling "systems"?
- What kind of systems are they?
- What are the positive/negative parts of the system?
- In what way am I out to change the status quo?
- What have the naysayers been saying about my work?
- Why did people say I would fail?

- Where was I and what happened when I hit the lowest moment of the journey in my project/research?

- Writing prompt: Which pictures and scenes come to mind when you think of important milestones in your work?

- Writing prompt: Tell the story of how you overcame one of your biggest obstacles so far?

- Writing prompt: What is it you didn't know about your subject matter when you set out? And how did you come to know it?

Thought-leadership writing and telling the truth

First-person articles in the thought-leadership style have parallels to service journalism and to solutions journalism, as mentioned in Chapter 2.

They are also akin to opinion writing and essay writing. Both are characterized by the author's strong voice and a quest to understand or explore an idea.

No matter what you call the type of writing, it must be truthful. Your truthfulness as an author is what gives your story legs and more importantly, truthfulness makes you and your story believable.

Similarly, your stories will not stand up if you are constantly trying to gloss over the negative, show off or simply look good. Doing so turns your stories into marketing copy.

More on the 17 types of thought-leadership writing

Let's drill down with a description of each of the 17 types of thought-leadership stories introduced in Chapter 4. I see this list and these definitions as fluid. If you've identified an additional type of story or have a suggestion on how to improve my definitions, please let me know.

Forward-looking stories

Best-practices stories

Best-practice stories break out and synthesize your hard-learned advice for your reader. You as the expert have seen people frequently making the mistakes you're addressing. You know because you made those same mistakes in the past, too. But now you're able to look back and better understand what went wrong.

These stories are of great service to the reader because their intent is to save others from the same pain and suffering you went through to learn what you know now.

Explore-the-solution stories

Explore-the-solution stories take the reader on a tour of a particular solution that is of interest to them and to you. It breaks down the solution and examines it from different vantages and viewpoints.

In addition to exploring the strengths and weaknesses of a given solution in your story, you can also consider the assumptions behind the solution. Done well, these stories show your audience the depth of your knowledge about your subject or research area. They serve the reader because you've done the hard work of synthesizing.

Applied-knowledge stories ("It's working there, why not try it here?" stories)

Applied-knowledge stories are stories in which you make a leap in thinking and take your reader along with you for that leap. You've noticed a solution working in one context? Then presuppose that it could work in another and write about it.

The writer walks the reader through what that solution applied in a different way could look like, exploring the potential pros and cons.

How-to-prevent-a-problem stories

How-to-prevent-a-problem stories, like best-practice stories, are a service to the reader because you are helping others avoid loss or trouble. In this case, you're using your insight to help readers avoid trouble before it happens.

Sometimes these stories explore the lesser-known problems that only a few are aware of because of their deep experience in their niche. The more interesting the problem, the more interesting the story here.

What-if stories

In what-if stories, the writer shows their ability to connect dots, see trends and imagine a particular future in a particular area. These stories can be fun, entertaining or outlandish, or they may have a serious tone.

The structure may set up one or more hypotheses, with the exposition focused on the impact that would be experienced should the scenario come true.

Explore-the-trends stories

Explore-the-trends stories walk the reader through what you determine are the trends in your niche. In these stories, the writer unpacks the trend, looking at why it's happening, why now, where it's happening, and what it may mean for the reader.

Impact-of-the trend stories

Impact-of-the trend stories explore how a trend is impacting something that is important to your audience.

Experts in a niche may see the impact of a trend more clearly than generalists because they see it happening consistently across the board. That allows the expert to provide an in-depth discussion of the impact.

By exploring the impact of a trend that matters greatly to the reader, you're helping them imagine possible outcomes they may be faced with down the road.

Retrospective thought-leadership stories

Understand-the-problem stories

Understand-the-problem stories take readers by the hand and guide them to a new level of clarity about a particular problem.

They synthesize evidence and opinion about the problem and present it in a form that makes it easier to grasp. These are not reports written by teams of experts. This is your view as a single expert who wants to share your take on the what, the how or the why of a problem.

Of course, a single expert's viewpoint on a complex problem can be very opinionated. Using first person and telling about your personal journey to understand the matter can make these stories more believable and more readable.

Reasons-why stories

Reasons-why stories, like understand-the-problem stories, explore the causes and roots of a problem. They are focused more on the causes than on the manifestation of the results.

In reasons-why stories, emerging thought leaders can unpack their understanding of a subject by constantly looking for a different, more accurate or more narrow reason behind a commonly held explanation. By breaking down causes and examining them from different viewpoints, the writer can help expand overall understanding of a problem.

Share-my-process stories

Share-my-process stories are extremely valuable, especially in times of great uncertainty. When calamity falls or a Black Swan event happens, sharing your process for meeting the challenge can come across as comforting and honest advice. It's clear that no one can know what will happen in such situations. As the emerging thought leader, you acknowledge that humbly and still try to serve by sharing what's working for you or others you are working with.

Similarly, when it's not a time of crisis or challenge, share-your-process stories serve your reader by presenting some of your best practices as a process.

Myth-buster stories

Myth-buster stories focus on detecting beliefs and ideas that you see as incorrect, unhelpful or baseless. Once you have identified a myth you'd like to debunk, you can explore how the myth took root, what's right about it, what's not so right about it, how you see it differently, or why you believe you're right.

Why-I-believe stories

Why-I-believe stories are an exposition on how you came to see the world or your niche, subject or research.

These can be deeply personal and include stories of your own transformation. Publishing such articles may feel risky because they capture a moment in time in the evolution of a belief you hold, and who knows if you'll hold that same belief tomorrow.

That's why these types of stories take courage, deep reflection and an ability to stare your own truth in the face. The act of writing such stories will certainly help you get clearer on your own beliefs.

I would suggest writing about a belief from which you currently have some distance. If you're currently going through a change in worldview, or you're still too close to a crisis that brought on a change in a belief, you may benefit from letting those ideas sit for a while before tackling a story about what happened and how it led to a new or evolved belief.

Personal-impact and personal-experience stories

Personal-impact and personal-experience stories share with readers how something changed you and why. Transformation is embedded in this story structure because you will have to share with your readers how you were before something happened or changed, and how you are now. In these stories, your readers can get to know you better by reliving with you an important experience you had.

What-really-happened stories

What-really-happened stories are like reason-why stories but are more focused on clarifying and setting straight a chain of events that may be misunderstood in your niche. This could be how something happened, why something is called the way it is, or your view on why something succeeded, failed or went wrong.

The focus here is on exploring events in sequence, and perhaps uncovering or clarifying other events to pull together a plausible explanation of what really happened.

What-surprised-me stories

What-surprised-me stories share with readers an aha or eye-opening moment you experienced. They show you as fallible and sincere, as you venture toward more understanding. These stories contrast your understanding before and after the aha moment, potentially busting some myths, or saving the reader time and pain by sharing your insight and how you gained it.

What-I-learned stories

What-I-learned stories are very similar to best-practices stories but are more retrospective in nature. They recount lessons learned, perhaps the hard way. These stories show the evolution in your understanding or explore individual aspects of your craft or research and how you came to know what you know. They are a place to give credit to others who helped you along your way.

Simplify-the-complex stories

Simplify-the-complex stories are stories that serve the reader by making something difficult to grasp much easier to do so.

These stories examine a complex subject and make it more accessible by breaking it down in new or different ways. They often benefit from good analogies and metaphors, as well as anecdotes, to illustrate the idea. If your audience constantly asks you about a complex subject, that might be a good subject to address in a simplify-the-complex story.

Types of stories and The Story-Framing System

By defining these types of stories, I want to help you start thinking about possible approaches for even more articles about your work. My hope is that in reading the section above, you already came up with new story ideas to add to your WIP list.

As mentioned, it's important to consider the type of story you want to write before generating your headlines using Step 5 of The Story-Framing System. When you keep these story types in mind, you'll generate better headlines, which in turn will help guide your writing and storytelling.

Fixes for "sins" in business writing

Now, I want to continue with the chart I began showing earlier when discussing the value of charts for brainstorming and keeping language parallel. The below is the full version of my brainstorming chart about "sins" in business writing.

These "sins" are problems I noticed over the years in stories I edited that were written by subject-matter experts for their companies.

The focus here is on the fix in column three. If you recognize that you're making one of these mistakes, consider the fix I propose. (See Figure 27.)

167

"Sins" and fixes in business writing (long version)

	"SIN" TYPE	A FIX
"Sins" of story angle	Author comes across as having nothing new to say	Find what's new about this topic. Go from the small to the large, or large to small to see it in a new perspective.
	Story is about a subject that is not really your business	Find a different story to tell.
	Basic idea of the story doesn't serve the reader	Bring in the readers' needs and pain points. What are the internal and external challenges the reader faces? Put them on a mind map.
	Story misses a chance to tell a bigger story	Consider the impact of the idea and the context of its origin. Do more to anchor your story in the larger scheme of things. In what way does your observation validate or debunk a wider trend?
	Story isn't memorable	Find a different way to tell the story.
	Story angle leads to wandering structure	Tighten the story structure.
	Story resulted from fuzzy thinking	Get clear on what you want to say by freewriting about it, getting interviewed or chartifying it.
	Article packs in too much	Have the courage needed to leave material on the cutting room floor.
	Story has a buried lead	Consider what's really new for the reader. What original view on the topic have you brought in? If it's not in the top three paragraphs, move it there and flip things around.
	"SIN" TYPE	A FIX
"Sins" of story execution	Repetition in a body of work (e.g., an article rehashes a study that someone could easily read themselves)	Look for ways to bring in opinion about existing ideas and concepts.
	Author is holding back their knowledge	Realize that it's hard to give away too much in short form, so start giving away your best ideas.
	Story has a slow start	Use the journalistic process of teasing out what's new in the lead to avoid an academic style with a preamble.
	Story talks down to the reader	Stand back and reconsider your audience and tone. Rewrite.

	"SIN" TYPE	A FIX
(continues)	Story moralizes	No one wants to hear from someone who is ranting and moralizing. Just stop it!
	Story states the known	Look for what's next or a new way to state what's already known that adds value and provides a unique perspective.
	Story includes mixed metaphors	Line up your metaphors and have a good laugh while you're doing so.
	Article is too long	Where can you synthesize and kick out material? Read a paragraph out loud. Summarize it out loud. Write down what you said.
	Story doesn't deliver on the headline	How would you like it if the dish you got at a restaurant was completely different than what you ordered? Tone down overly ambitious headlines or improve the article to make sure deliver on your headline.
	Story includes incomplete disclosure of source materials	Go back and capture your sources. Create a system for doing it so that it doesn't become a big problem shortly before you're ready to publish.
	No human face on the story	How can a character, example or anecdote bring your story to life?
	Article exaggerates the truth	Remember, you're trying to build trust with your writing.
	Examples aren't uniform or don't make the point intended in the story	Break out your examples and examine them outside of your narrative, for instance by capturing them in a chart. Do they hold up? If not, find new ones or leave them out.
	Story has one example, and then you claim it's a trend	Resist the urge to name a new trend based on very early observation and incomplete information. Consider posing the idea as a question instead.
	Parts of the story are dishonest or questionable	Just don't do it!
	Piece is too critical of the competition	Business writing is not the place for rival-bashing.
	You're afraid to talk about mistakes in the article when they were an important part of the story	We are all human and stories benefit from showing your vulnerability.

(continues)	Article includes questionable or sloppy statistics	Do the legwork to get the right statistics or leave them out. Adding a statistic doesn't make you smart if it's not bringing the story forward.
	Story sells something old as a new idea	This is a bit like click bait. It's very disappointing in the end. If you're claiming an idea is new, make sure it is.
	Article compares apples to oranges.	Logic must prevail. Don't try to slip this one by your reader or you will lose trust.
	Story tries too hard	Stand back, relax, and rewrite from the top in simpler language. You're the expert. You don't have to bring every single proof point to be believed. Show the reader the big picture.
	Story has old examples, no examples, or no data	Do the legwork needed to bring in the right examples or data.

Figure 27—"Sins" and fixes in business writing (long version)

Writing by an expert for a general audience— Michael's Buyer's Bench piece

Here I'd like to introduce you to Michael Parker, an American colleague of mine in Frankfurt. Michael and I are both in the Professional Speakers Club of Frankfurt. Michael, a coach and trainer, earned a doctorate in religious studies at Yale University.

Below you will see Michael's unedited version of a story written to explain a process in sales. Then you will see my edits. Michael was kind enough to let me show the "before/after" versions of his story for this book.

This example shows how a different set up for a story can bring in more tension and make it a more interesting read.

Michael's original:

The Buyer's Bench

The goal of pitching is to "sell your ideas." But pitching isn't selling in the usual sense of the word. Selling is about getting someone to "buy" your product or service. The goal of pitching is to get "buy-in" for your idea.* So, what is buy-in?

One way to think of it is in terms of the so-called "buyer's bench." The buyer's bench represents the stages people go through before they are ready to commit to your idea. These stages are: awareness, understanding, acceptance and (finally) buy-in.

People first must become aware of your idea. You may have the world's greatest idea, but if people aren't aware of it ... well, it's dead in the water. Once people become aware of your idea, however, they still might not understand it. If they don't, you need to explain it to them in terms they can understand. But even if your audience understands your idea, they still might not be ready to accept it. In that case, you are going to have to give them a "nudge" to move them along the bench from "acceptance" to "buy-in" i.e. to approval, adoption and commitment.

So, when people buy-into your idea, they understand it, they accept it and they are willing to commit to making it happen. It is no longer just your idea. It is now their idea too.

Last year, I did fundraising for a nonprofit organization, which is well known throughout the United

---

* I owe this formulation to my friend and colleague, Chris W.

States and many other English-speaking countries, but not very well known in Europe.

Initially, I tried to "sell" local companies on the idea of sponsoring our annual conference, but in talking to them, I soon realized many of them were completely unaware of the existence of our club and its mission. They were at the "low end" of the buyer's bench. In order to get their buy-in for the idea of sponsorship, I first had to "move" them "up" the bench, a step at a time. First, I had to make them aware of the existence of our organization. Second, I had to give them some understanding of our mission and purpose. Third, I had to win their acceptance for my idea by linking our organization's purpose and mission to their fund-raising goals. Finally, after they accepted the idea of sponsorship, I had to provide them reasons to actually commit to it and to fund the project: I had to get their "buy-in".

So, no matter how compelling your idea, if you want to "sell" it, you first need to locate your audience on the "buyer's bench" and determine what they need to know (think and feel) in order to move successively "up" the bench to "buy-into" your idea.

As Seth Godin says, "It's not about great ideas, it's about selling those ideas and making them happen". In other words, it's about getting buy-in from the people who can turn your idea into a reality.

Here are my suggestions for edits and a slight re-structure of Michael's text. Below that, you'll see the final version without the markup.

The Buyer's Bench

Last year I did fundraising for a non-profit which is well known throughout the United States and many other English-speaking countries, but not very well known in Europe.

Initially, I tried to "sell" local companies in Germany on the idea of sponsoring our annual conference, but in talking to them, I soon realized many of them were completely unaware of the existence of our club and its mission.

I realized they were at the "low end" of the buyer's bench.

The buyer's bench?

What's that?

The buyer's bench represents the stages people go through before they are ready to commit to your idea. These stages are: awareness, understanding, acceptance and (finally) buy-in.

~~The goal of pitching is to "sell your ideas'. But pitching isn't selling in the usual sense of the word. Selling is about getting someone to "buy" your product or service. The goal of pitching is to get "buy in" for your idea.*~~

~~So, what is *buy in*?~~

~~One way to think of it is in terms of the so-called "buyer's bench". The buyer's bench represents the stages people go through before they are ready to commit to your idea. These stages are awareness, understanding, acceptance and (finally) buy-in.~~

People first must become aware of your idea. You may have the world's greatest idea, but if people aren't aware of it ... well, it's dead in the water. Once ~~people become~~ <u>they are</u> aware ~~of your idea~~, however, they still might not understand it. If they don't, you need to explain it to them in terms they can understand.

But even if your audience understands your idea, they still might not be ready to accept it. In that case, you are going to have to give them a "nudge" to move them along the bench from "acceptance" to "buy-in" <u>-</u> i.e. to approval, adoption and commitment.

So, when people *buy-into* your idea, they understand it, they accept it and they are willing to commit to making it happen. It is no longer just your idea. It is now their idea<u>,</u> too.

~~Last year I did fundraising for a non-profit organization, which is well-known throughout the United States and many other English-speaking countries, but not very well known in Europe.~~

~~Initially, I tried to "sell" local companies on the idea of sponsoring our annual conference, but in talking to them, I soon realized many of them were completely unaware of the existence of our club and its mission. They were at the "low end" of the buyer's bench.~~

In order to get their buy-in for the idea of sponsorship, I first had to "move" them "up" the bench, a step at a time.

First, I had to make them aware of the existence of our organization. Second, I had to give them some understanding of our mission and purpose. Third, I had to win their acceptance for my idea by linking our organization's purpose and mission to their ~~fundraising~~

gifting goals. Finally, after they accepted the idea of sponsorship, I had to provide them reasons to actually commit to it and to fund the project: I had to get their "buy-in".

So, no matter how compelling your idea, if you want to "sell" it, you first need to locate your audience on the "buyer's bench" and determine what they need to know (think and feel) in order to move successively "up" the bench to "buy-into" your idea.

As marketing expert Seth Godin says, "It's not about great ideas, it's about selling those ideas and making them happen.". In other words, it's about getting *buy-in* from the people who can turn your idea into a reality.

~~*I owe this formulation to my friend and colleague, Chris W.~~

Here is the final edited version:

The Buyer's Bench

Last year I did fundraising for a non-profit which is well known throughout the United States and many other English-speaking countries, but not very well known in Europe.

Initially, I tried to "sell" local companies in Germany on the idea of sponsoring our annual conference, but in talking to them, I soon realized many of them were completely unaware of the existence of our club and its mission.

I realized they were at the "low end" of the buyer's bench.

The buyer's bench?

What's that?

The buyer's bench represents the stages people go through before they are ready to commit to your idea. These stages are: awareness, understanding, acceptance and (finally) buy-in.

People first must become aware of your idea. You may have the world's greatest idea, but if people aren't aware of it ... well, it's dead in the water. Once they are aware, however, they still might not understand it. If they don't, you need to explain it to them in terms they can understand.

But even if your audience understands your idea, they still might not be ready to accept it. In that case, you are going to have to give them a "nudge" to move them along the bench from "acceptance" to "buy-in" - i.e. to approval, adoption and commitment.

So, when people *buy-into* your idea, they understand it, they accept it and they are willing to commit to making it happen. It is no longer just your idea. It is now their idea, too.

In order to get their buy-in for the idea of sponsorship, I first had to "move" them "up" the bench, a step at a time.

First, I had to make them aware of the existence of our organization. Second, I had to give them some understanding of our mission and purpose. Third, I had to win their acceptance for my idea by linking our organization's purpose and mission to their gifting goals. Finally, after they accepted the idea of sponsorship, I had to provide them reasons to actually commit to it and to fund the project: I had to get their "buy-in".

> So, no matter how compelling your idea, if you want to "sell" it, you first need to locate your audience on the "buyer's bench" and determine what they need to know (think and feel) in order to move successively "up" the bench to "buy-into" your idea.
>
> As marketing expert Seth Godin says, "It's not about great ideas, it's about selling those ideas and making them happen." In other words, it's about getting *buy-in* from the people who can turn your idea into a reality.

An article written in the thought-leadership style

Let's look at an article I would describe as one written in the thought-leadership style.

It is written in first person, it shares a process with readers, and the story is useful and actionable.

At the same time, the story is free of marketing and salesy language, and there is no reference to the services offered by the author, Denise Withers. Denise has separated her offering from her story so that the article does not turn into marketing copy.

Denise is a story coach and consultant and does story work within companies. Here she gives away her knowledge for free, but most likely, readers will still need outside help if they want to try it themselves.

My thanks to Denise for allowing me to reprint her article here.

In my comments, I explain what I think works well in Denise's piece.

Headline: **Improve operations with story circles**

Her headline is very descriptive and short

Sub-head: **Part of the Leaders' Rapid Response Tools Series #LeadRRT**

Other options:
-How story circles can improve your operations
-How story circles generate new ideas for operations in your company
-How story circles spark new approaches

By: **Denise Withers**

Date: **April 13, 2020**

Lede/Lead-in: Things are changing so fast that leaders and managers need to adapt their operations almost daily. At the same time, they have to find ways to keep their people engaged amid on-going churn.

One of the most powerful tools I use to help clients lead through change like this is a simple story circle. Here's how it works.

She gets to the point **fast**

Set-up

Start by scheduling some kind of a regular check-in with your team. You can do this face-to-face, or via technology, using video, audio, chats, email or even a Google Form.

She **starts from the beginning**

Then, before the first session, spend a bit of prep time helping your people understand what a story is and how to tell one simply. At its core, every story describes the way someone solves a problem or meets a goal. The stories can be as short or as long as you want to make them—most can be told in under a minute. To keep this brief, when they're sharing stories, try to have them do it in just three bullet points:

She **shares her philosophy/ viewpoint**

- What I was trying to do (the problem)
- What actually happened (the quest)
- How things turned out (the solution)

She **gives you something useful** that you can take directly into your next team meeting

Facilitation

During every check-in, ask each person the same questions.

Tell us about one thing that worked well (WWW—what worked well).

> She makes it **easy to remember**

Tell us how we could make one thing even better. (EBI—even better if).

> Again - It's easy to remember

This wording is critical, as it keeps the focus positive. Rather than opening the door for people to spew out a list of what's broken, it invites them to generate useful suggestions for improvements. Make sure they follow the story structure and don't just give 2–3 word answers that only give you the outcome. "I made 3 sales" isn't going to be helpful. This might be a hard habit for people to break, as we're used to only reporting outcomes. But the real gold of stories is found during the quest, where you discover what people try or do to overcome obstacles. So encourage your team to acknowledge the obstacles. It's only by showing us how they worked through them that we can see what heroes they are!

> She **tells you why** her approach makes sense

> She uses **first-person** – that makes her accessible

> She uses **interesting** language

> She uses **the language of the niche she's writing about**

> Exclamations are not my favorite

Analysis

Once the group finishes sharing their stories, you have several options. You can analyze them as a group or on you own. Either way, the process is the same.

First, you look for patterns. Are several people experiencing the same things? If so, what does that mean? And how can you address it? If you find a pattern in the "what worked well" stories, then you've identified a core

> She tells you to analyze and then tells you how to analyze

strength that you can build on to address issues elsewhere in your work or organization.

Then, you review the EBI stories. Inviting people to suggest improvements is a fantastic way to seed innovation. Even if their ideas don't work for the initial problem, they might be perfect for another problem somewhere else in the organization.

> She talks about the benefits of her approach

For example, I worked with an organization that implemented story circles via Google Forms. They decided only to focus on "what worked well" stories—and to integrate it into their performance improvement and communications systems. Every time an employee experienced success or a win, she submitted the story. Her manager was automatically notified, which triggered a follow up conversation to celebrate. And the Communications team reached out to see if this was a story they could share in their internal or external products. The benefit for performance was that it shifted reviews from a once a year event that everyone dreaded, to an on-going, appreciative conversation to help employees continually develop. And the comms people loved it, because it was always so hard for them to find success stories to share.

> She tells a story from her own practice

> More benefits

Scaling

Story circles are most powerful if you can embed them across the organization. Building on a process called Most Significant Change, you can set up a story chain that feeds intel, insights and ideas up, through and across the organization. One person takes responsibility for each story circle or node, choosing

> She clearly has done this at companies, or she wouldn't know anything about scaling her method

the most important or significant stories to share. This synthesis process continues up the hierarchy or across the matrix, with one person at each level short-listing or synthesizing the key stories to share.

> She explains how it works

If your group is too big to share stories in a live meeting, you can have them do it via something simple like a Google Form. The form should contain the two questions. When people fill it in, the form automatically populates a spreadsheet, creating an instant story database for further analysis and action.

> Pretty cool idea!

Benefits

> Her sub-heads are labels – I prefer phrases

Sharing stories like this isn't just good for continuous improvement. It has several benefits for your team as well.

> This ties back into her initial focus on operations

It offers them a chance to connect and develop stronger relationships with each other.

It shows them that you're listening and you care.

It creates learning opportunities across departments and roles.

> She uses **repetitive language for effect**

It develops reflective practice skills for on-going improvement.

It engages them, by making them feel more in control of their work.

> She drives the point home again – this can be done without a big technology investment
>
> Of course, you'll need her to help you do it

Story circles cost nothing but time and can pay off in big dividends. Give it a try at the end of this week. You'll be blown away by the results.

> She doesn't just say give it a try – she says do it this week

> This is the payoff she promotes

> She accomplishes all this in **874 words**

https://medium.com/@denisewithers/improve-operations-with-story-circles-e62125040092

181

Key takeaways

- Thought-leadership writing often includes stories of transformation related to your work.
- Many people look to thought leaders to express hard truths about the subject at hand.
- The 17 types of thought-leadership articles can be used in a body of short-form work or as part of long-form writing.
- When subject-matter experts write for a general audience, they often make the same mistakes in their writing, regardless of the area of expertise. There are fixes for the "sins" of business writing.

CHAPTER 8

Finding the Courage and Confidence to Write

"A MIND ONCE STRETCHED BY A NEW IDEA NEVER
REGAINS ITS ORIGINAL DIMENSIONS"
—OLIVER WENDELL HOLMES

Sharing your views and opinions in writing is a courageous act that makes most people uncomfortable, even experts who have come up in academia and are accustomed to banging out research papers for publication.

Writing in the first person for a general audience about your own opinions, observations and experiences means you won't necessarily have the extra layer of "protection" provided to you by co-authors and editors, or by the research itself.

I, too, felt resistance to blogging about my work. I only published my first articles about my own work and ideas a few years back, although I had thousands of journalistic articles to my name by that time. It took some time and nudges from my project editors for me to find the right voice and get more comfortable with writing about my own opinions.

Everyone faces some internal resistance, and getting started is one of the most difficult steps in writing. But after you have managed to get going, writing feels so much easier. Then you've got forward momentum. The ball is rolling.

Finishing your work is also a great feeling. Often, the act of finishing is about announcing that your work has reached the "good enough" marker. It is perfectionism that keeps many from every publishing a word. That's why I recommend using "good enough" as your benchmark.

You will need tenacity to finish because it's so easy to bog in the middle—for days, weeks or even years, as you listen to the judge in your head who says you cannot do it or what you've written isn't good enough. I say you can and should finish your work. Arriving at the finish line is an amazing feat and an amazing feeling. It's worth the pain and suffering you will experience along the way.

Here are some of my tips, collected over the years, that will help you avoid procrastination, focus on your writing and make your writing more impactful.

Clear the decks

For many people, the hardest part of writing is getting started in a meaningful way. Know that writing often happens in spurts. If you know you need to make progress, start clearing time in your schedule and space in your mind for a spurt to manifest. In other words, clear the decks.

To make that spurt happen, cancel appointments, search for quiet, get the minimum done elsewhere to tie up loose ends. This isn't the time to start other new projects as a way of avoiding the task at hand. Sticky-note the phrase "postpone it purposefully" to your monitor. Now, it's time to focus.

Bust your blockades

To write better and produce more word volume, clean up the non-writing areas of your life.

If you are stuck in one area of your life, that can lead to being stuck in another unrelated area. I believe this is about energy. When you manage to free up energy by taking responsibility for something you had been avoiding, or making a change that was long needed, that energy cycles back to you in the form of creativity and writing productivity. Doing the right thing and making hard decisions in your personal or work life can lead to great bursts of positive energy that will translate into more writing and more fluid writing.

Find an embodiment

Find an embodiment of the power you need before each writing session.

I have built this into most of my workdays, even when I'm not writing that day. Standing near my desk, I make a motion with my arms and legs that is an embodiment of a feeling or idea. I got this idea from the creator of the Emotional Dance Process, Tiamat Ohm.

Often, I stand and make the motion that Mr. Miyagi instructed his student Daniel to do in the film "The Karate Kid." Miyagi was teaching Daniel principles of karate and life by making him put wax onto cars using his right hand and wipe the wax off with his left hand. The instruction was "Wax on and wax off. Wax on and wax off." As I stand there repeating Mr. Miyagi's instructions in my head, I make the motion with my arms. This ritual helps ground me and helps me visualize what I'm doing and why.

Writing is a process like waxing on and waxing off. It takes focus and dedication, and it's essentially repetitive in nature. Similarly, just when you think a piece is ready, it might need some more "wax on, wax off" treatment. That's where getting some distance from what you have written can help. When you return to the piece, you'll know if what it needs is more or less waxing.

See it as a hero's journey for yourself

Understand that writing comes with ups and downs.

Like a hero's journey, when you embark on writing a piece, you'll inevitably hit challenges along the way. Some will be real, and some will be imagined, courtesy of the judge in your head who supplies a constant stream of criticism if you let him.

Know that these challenges are built into the process and that you can come out whole and more mature on the other side, despite how difficult it might feel during the process.

Create arbitrary urgency

If no boss or editor is breathing down your neck to finish a piece, it can be easy to let stories drag on for a long time. To just get your article written, build urgency into your process, whether that urgency is real or arbitrary.

I have heard people say that the cadence of the content is more important than its quality when it comes to social media marketing. Stick to your chosen cadence and get your article done in time, even if no authority figure is making you do it. Your own deadline is a real deadline. Make it an urgent priority.

Print a lot

Print, read, mark up. Repeat.

I rarely send off a piece of writing for a client without having printed it first. When I see my work on the printed page, I see it differently than I do on the screen. I inevitably discover mistakes I had overlooked, and I can assess the flow and rhythm in the writing better when I view it on the printed page. For shorter pieces, I also recommend reading it aloud, especially in the places you feel the writing may bog down. You'll be better able to sense the cadence and rhythm in the piece, or the lack thereof.

Speak to an inanimate object as if it's human

Find an object of interest and start talking to it about the task at hand.

Got any hills or mountains near where you live? Speak to one and say, "Mountain, I'm going to climb you." Announce your writing intent to the object of your choice.

Do for yourself what you would do for others

If you've ever done amazing feats for someone else at home or at work, make it your turn this time. Put the same enormous energy into your project that you already showed you could muster for someone else.

Join a speechmaking club and start writing your own speeches

Join Toastmasters or the likes to help you get more words on paper in the form of speeches.

A speechmaking club will get you writing more and give you external deadlines for that writing. Writing speeches is great practice for writing articles in first-person, since speeches must be conversational.

Join a writing community

Writing doesn't have to be a solo sport. If you want to feel less alone in the process, find a writing group that works for you.

If you're being asked to write regularly for work, consider organizing your own company writing session with colleagues within work hours or shortly before your day begins. If done virtually, participants can announce their writing task at the beginning of the session, go on mute, leave cameras on and all write simultaneously.

Learn from improv theater

An enormous number of lessons from improvisation theater apply to writing.

You've got to "establish the relationship" with a scene partner at the very beginning of a scene. Similarly, as a writer, you need to quickly establish your relationship with your reader by showing that you, as the writer, understand the reader.

Improv also teaches players to say "yes, and" when creating a scene and receiving an "offer" from another actor. In freewriting, you're following the flow of your ideas. When an idea arrives in your mind, you say to it "yes, and" and you keep writing to find out where that next "and" is going to take you.

Need to deepen a story you're working on or not quite sure what to say next? Then do a digression and add something that amounts to saying "I believe" in a scene. Similarly, actors are taught to bring in "remember when" scenes to deepen their improvisation pieces. In your writing, do a quick look back at something to give it some "historical" perspective.

Document your research and idea-development process

Record your own process of researching and reporting for yourself or for possible use in a narrative about your work. What did you think, feel, hear, smell or taste along the way as you were uncovering your subject matter and assimilating the knowledge you're sharing?

The "where" and the "when" of your process are important as well. Where were you and when did a particular realization or point of insight come? Record these stories so you can share them later.

Capture along the way

Set up and use an effective capture method for your ideas and research that allows you to easily follow your tracks and find a particular piece of input once again quickly and easily.

Since I listen to a lot of audio books and podcasts while driving, I have created a "messages to myself" group on the messaging app I use. I speak notes to myself into the chat. It's also possible to have those audio notes turned to text.

Another suggestion: Keep a pen and paper by your bed to capture your dream world and look for clues manifested by your subconscious about what's really going on in your life and work. You could even get a pen with a little light on it so that you don't have to turn on a big light to do some scribbling in the night.

Do nothing

If you're stuck with a writing project and have been trying for a long time to find the way forward, the best thing may be to do nothing. Just take a break.

Move on to other projects, change settings, take a walk or bake cookies. That may be all you need to tackle the writing with fresh eyes.

Change locations for sprints

A writing retreat doesn't have to be far from home for it to be effective. I have frequently gone to a vacation rental in my own city to get a change of scenery and work on a particular writing task. While you're there, if you're wasting time and doing the wrong tasks first, your imminent return becomes like a ticking clock. You start saying to yourself, "Oh, no, I've only got X number of days left here and I need to get Y written!"

If you can't get away, sometimes just changing writing locations within your home or office makes a world of difference. If you're facing writer's block at your desk, move to your couch or dining room table. If you're on your sofa already, move to a desk or sit outside in the fresh air. Different environments offer different perspectives and can get you out of a mental block or rut.

Peel back your layers of armor to access your genius

Get real, truthful, open and honest with yourself as part of your work process.

Good writing shares truths and understandings from life and work. To be generating these constantly, you've got to make it a practice to be unearthing them from within yourself. Be vulnerable with others and painfully honest with yourself. That will help you see your subject matter in new and different ways.

Keep your biases in check

Listen to the critics, but mostly to the critics close to you. Those are the critics who really care about you. If critics close to you say some of your biases are rearing their heads, then take note.

We all have biases but they're one of the hardest things to see in ourselves. If you've uncovered some of yours in the past that you'd rather not have, learn to keep those biases in check. Just like you're on the lookout for a particular word that you habitually misspell or use incorrectly, be on the lookout for biases in your writing.

Have the courage to leave it out

As an expert, you likely collect reams and reams of information relevant to your subject. In the end, it's not all going to be usable in a book or article. Nonetheless, many of us feel a certain responsibility to people we have interviewed or a certain need to make sure a point gets its due mention.

In the end, it takes courage to leave out material, to leave reel on the cutting room floor as filmmakers used to do. It's not easy to kick out your ideas. My suggestion is to resist the urge to pack it all in so you don't have to cut too much.

If you're working on a book, then what you're thinking of squeezing in can possibly go in an article related to the book. If you're working on an article, well, there will always be another article you can write.

Look for circular stories

Close your circles in life and writing. As a journalist, one structure I learned for feature writing was the circular structure or wrapping back to an idea you introduced in the beginning.

In life, it's fascinating to observe how you or others "come full circle" through a transformation, or an event or an object seems to reappear or "overlap" at an opportune time. Be on the lookout for ways to wrap back and pick up your readers in your writing.

Pack your facts and figures into a tidy area

As a subject-matter expert, you know a lot, but the goal of writing is not to put your knowledge on show.

The goal of your writing should be to serve the reader by helping them survive or thrive in some way as a result of reading your work. As such, if you need facts and figures to back up your point, consider packing them into a consolidated section that hard-core readers can dig through, and others can skim if they wish.

To decide if a fact or figure should be included or not, ask yourself "Does this bring the story forward?" That's what filmmakers ask themselves when considering every scene and detail in their final cut—does this bring the story forward? If it doesn't, leave out your fact or figure.

Be appropriate

Freewriting is the place to regurgitate the thoughts on your mind that are wicked, nasty, hateful, snide, revengeful or lewd. It's the place to let it all hang out. If you want to do a striptease of your thoughts, that's where you go to do it. You're in private.

But in thought-leadership writing, we need to mind our manners.

Yes, we need to write from life and from our experience, but we also need to use our feeling for and understanding of our audience to write those things that will resonate with them and not make readers uncomfortable.

I once heard something that has stuck in my mind, which I call the "Jackie Kennedy fashion test." Someone said that Jackie did all women a favor by creating a fashion benchmark. Women, and men for that fact, too, can ask themselves the Jackie fashion question: "What would Jackie wear?" The answer was always the same: Jackie would wear what was appropriate.

What should you write? You should write what's appropriate. This doesn't mean your writing cannot be controversial or thought provoking, pushing the bar ever further. Writing well means being tactful.

Identify your protagonist and antagonist, even in nonfiction

One of my editors for this book, Patti McCracken, encouraged me to identify the protagonist and antagonist in my story. Yes, even nonfiction explanatory books like this one should have them.

In my case, my antagonist is bad writing, in particular bad story angles. My protagonist is story framing and my five-step method for creating better story angles.

Guide the child

Patti also told me to write as if I were guiding a child. That was not meant as an insult to my readers. She meant I should write with a teacherly but personable voice and explain things as simply as possible. Basically, she suggested acting as a gentle leader, taking readers by the hand and showing them my viewpoint on what works in my subject area.

Trust yourself

Writing is also a process of finding out what you think. Trust yourself and the hunch you have that you're on to something good and your ideas need to be uncovered, explained and understood.

What you have to say is valuable and necessary. Believe in that and share your ideas.

Key takeaways

- Writing takes courage, even for experts.
- Getting started and finishing are some of the hardest parts of writing, but it's worth the journey.
- To write well and with impact, become a student of your subject matter and also of yourself.

Acknowledgements

I would like to acknowledge the following people for making a positive contribution to my life and work over the years: Mom, Dad, Brook, Isabella, Colette, Christiane, Birgit, Almuth, Moritz, Carmen and Manuel. I'd also like to acknowledge many of my teachers and professors from the past: The late Rosemary Monferdini, Mrs. Thorpe, the late Mary Beth Perkins, the late Ted Cron and Tina Rosenberg. As well, a special thanks to my late editor Catherine Downing, to Geni Certain and to Chris Waddle, all of The Anniston Star. Finally, a thank you to my editors at Dow Jones, Ellen Thalman and Adam Najberg.

Book and General Credits

Reporting and research
Robin Athey
Michael Parker
Stuart McCalla
Tina Nazarian

Concept development
James McCabe
Stefanie Nürnberger

Editing and proofreading
Patti McCracken
Maria Atanasov
Michael Denzin

Art, design, images and production
Nicolás Concha Roa
Jill Ronsley
Kerstin Langer
Manjit Jari

Marketing and sales
Nicolás Concha Roa
Nadia Fyvie-Feldmann
Natalia Skoczylas
Jane Wesman

General/Business Support
Alma Quiroga
Pedro Malaga
Sebastian Saavedra-Reib

References

References are listed in no particular order.

"Lend Me Your Ears: All You Need to Know about Making Speeches and Presentations": Max Atkison; Random House, 2004.

"Think for Yourself: Restoring Common Sense in an Age of Experts and Artificial Intelligence": Vikram Mansharamani; Harvard Business Review Press, 2020.

"Everybody Writes: Your Go-To Guide to Creating Ridiculously Good Content": Ann Handley; John Wiley and Sons Inc., 2014.

"Accidental Genius: Using Writing to Generate Your Best Ideas, Insight, and Content": Mark Levy; Berrett-Koehler Publishers, 2010.

"Thought Leaders: How to Capture, Package and Deliver Your Ideas for Greater Commercial Success": Matt Church, Scott Stein, Michael Henderson; Harper Collins, 2011.

"Amplifiers: The Power of Motivational Leadership to Inspire and Influence": Matt Church; Matt Church Pty Ltd., 2020.

"Conceptual Blockbusting: A Guide to Better Ideas": James L. Adams; Basic Books, 1969.

"Turning Pro; Steven Pressfield": Black Irish Books, 2012.

"Reframing: The art of thinking differently": Karim Benammar; Uitgeverij Boom, 2012.

"The Net and the Butterfly: The Art and Practice of Breakthrough Thinking": Olivia Fox Cabane, Judah Pollack; Portfolio, 2017.

"Escape from the Ivory Tower: A Guide to Making Your Science Matter": Nancy Baron, Liz Neeley (Contributor); Island Press, 2010.

"Pitch Anything: An Innovative Method for Presenting, Persuading, and Winning the Deal": Oren Klaff; McGraw-Hill Education, 2011.

"The Thought Leaders Practice": Matt Church, Peter Cook (Contributor), Scott Stein (Contributor); Thought Leaders, 2016.

"Writing to Persuade: How to Bring People Over to Your Side": Trish Hall; Liveright Publishing, 2019.

"The Creative Habit: Learn It and Use It for Life": Twyla Tharp; Simon Schuster, 2006.

"Seven Stages: Story and the Human Experience": Joe Lambert; Digital Diner Press, 2013.

"Writing for Story: Craft Secrets of Dramatic Nonfiction": Jon Franklin; Plume, 1986.

"The Writer's Journey: Mythic Structure for Writers": Christopher Vogler; Michael Wiese Productions, 1998.

"Storycraft: The Complete Guide to Writing Narrative Nonfiction": Jack R. Hart; University of Chicago Press, 2011.

"The Creative Attitude: Learning to Ask and Answer the Right Questions": Roger C. Schank, Peter G Childers; MacMillan, 1988.

"Find Your Why: A Practical Guide to Discovering Purpose for You and Your Team": Simon Sinek, David Mead, Peter Docker; Portfolio, 2017.

"Your Best Year Ever: A 5-Step Plan for Achieving Your Most Important Goals": Michael Hyatt; Baker Books, 2018.

"Ready to Be a Thought Leader: How to Increase Your Influence, Impact, and Success": Denise Brosseau, Guy Kawasaki; Jossey-Bass, 2013.

"The Art and Craft of Feature Writing": William Blundell; Plume, 1988.

PRAISE FOR
RHEA'S WORKSHOPS ON IDEATION, MESSAGING, VALUE ARTICULATION AND WRITING

"Your workshop showed me that I should invest more time not only thinking about ideas, but also on how to wrap them into a nice story."
Jana (Consultant)

"We had ample chances to express ourselves as well as to grasp all others' views, and we received personalized input from three different coaches in various formats. Rhea, you touched me because I felt heard by you and you took time to think about your input for me."
Vero (Scientist)

"Your workshop helped me so much in getting clarity about what makes me different from others. Learning about thought leadership and especially how to write like one gave me so many 'aha' moments."
Miriam (Independent business owner)

"Your workshop made me more confident in my writing and my belief that storytelling elements are vital for scientific discourse."
Marius (Scientist)

"This was the first time writing stories felt easy for me."
Bettina (Lawyer and mediator)

"Now I dig deeper with my writing. I have become mindful of when I am not thinking deeply enough."
Gretchen (Founder, finance company)

"Rhea's workshops provided an approachable framework that helped me clarify my goals and sort out what I have to say that, from my unique perspective, adds value."
Candice (Sustainability Communications)

"Your workshop was a lot of food for thought and it was impressive how fast we moved forward."
Winfried (Finance professional)

**Get a proposal for workshops at your company.
Contact us today at:
team@instituteforthoughtleadership.com**

Printed in Great Britain
by Amazon

86433756R00122